STARGÅTE

SG·1 ™

THE ILLUSTRATED COMPANION
SEASON 10

STARGATE SG-1: THE ILLUSTRATED COMPANION SEASON 10

ISBN-10: 1 84576 311 4
ISBN-13: 9781845763114

Published by
Titan Books
A division of
Titan Publishing Group Ltd
144 Southwark St
London
SE1 0UP

First edition January 2008
2 4 6 8 10 9 7 5 3 1

DEDICATION
For Grandma Nora.

ACKNOWLEDGEMENTS
First, I would like to thank all the cast and crew of *Stargate SG-1* who have always given up their time for me —
whether on the phone, in-between takes on set, or in their trailers whilst having a rushed dinner. They're truly a
wonderful bunch of people and they made every interview a delight. Special thanks go to Chris Judge for his
thoughtful Foreword and to Brad Wright and Robert C. Cooper for their eloquent Afterword. Big thanks to Brigitte
Prochaska and Carole Appleby in the press office for setting everything up, especially during my much-loved set
visits, and to Karol Mora whose help and support made this book far easier to compile. Huge thanks must go to the
lovely Sharon Gosling for stepping in to write some pieces for me at the last minute — I owe you one. And of course,
thanks to Jo Boylett, my editor, whose patience seems to know no bounds!

Titan Books would like to thank all the *Stargate SG-1* cast and crew, in particular those who kindly wrote pieces
for this book. Many thanks also to James Robbins for supplying us (once again!) with wonderful production art.
And last, but definitely not least, thank you to Karol Mora at MGM for your continuing help.

To receive advance information, news, competitions, and exclusive Titan offers online,
please register as a member by clicking the "sign up" button on our website: **www.titanbooks.com**
Did you enjoy this book? We love to hear from our readers. Please e-mail us at:
readerfeedback@titanemail.com or write to Reader Feedback at the above address.

Visit our website: **www.titanbooks.com**

A CIP catalogue record for this title is available from the British Library.

Printed and bound in the United States of America.

STARGÅTE
SG·1 ™

THE ILLUSTRATED COMPANION
SEASON 10

Natalie Barnes
with Sharon Gosling

Stargate SG-1 developed for television by
Brad Wright & Jonathan Glassner

TITAN BOOKS

Contents

Foreword

t is a cold, blustery, rainy day in the middle of August in Vancouver, or, as we like to call it, summer. It is one day before this foreword is due and I feel the weight of the world on my shoulders. Okay, maybe not the world but at least Brigitte, our lovely publicist, who has been charged with the daunting task of making sure I have this foreword completed on time. As I sit here in front of my trusty typewriter – I mean computer – ever-present friend Scotch by my side, cigar smoldering in the ashtray, I am consumed by one nagging question: Why have I, Christopher Judge, been asked to write the foreword for *Stargate SG-1: The Illustrated Companion Season 10* – the last, and possibly most important foreword thus far? And let me clarify. I say "most important" out of no sense of self-grandiosity (it is so a word!), but simply from the undeniable fact that this being the last *Stargate SG-1 Illustrated Companion* foreword that will ever be written, it must not only introduce the tenth and final season, but also provide a certain amount of closure to the previous guides.

Wait a minute… now that I think about it, that burden would probably fall on the shoulders of the writers of the afterword! And talk about a hedge. In case this foreword stinks, the Grand Poo-bahs themselves, executive producers Brad Wright and Robert Cooper, are writing the afterword. The pressure is gone. Okay, maybe it was gas, but all of a sudden I have a very bearable lightness of being, realizing I do not have to provide closure at all! All I have to do is introduce the *Season 10 Illustrated Companion*.

So, back to that nagging question. Why was I asked to write this foreword? After much soul-searching (well, I call it soul-searching, you may call it reviewing previous *Illustrated Companion* forewords), the answer to this question has hit me like a staff blast. I am the last person to be affiliated with the show from the very beginning who can actually say, "I've never written a foreword before!" So here I am. And I have to tell you that season ten really took us all on a rollercoaster ride of emotions. From incredible highs, shooting the absolutely magical two hundredth episode and knowing that we would be forever immortalized in the *Guinness World Records* book, to the gut-wrenching lows of learning we had been cancelled, and that heartbreaking walk with Amanda, Michael, Ben and Claudia, up the ramp and through the Stargate on Stage Five for the final time.

And through it all YOU were there. You, our fans! In 1997, you were there. And a full decade later you are still here, your voices still being heard loud and clear. So whether you are a Shipper, Slasher, or whatever, and wherever in the 150 countries that *Stargate SG-1* is broadcast you live… We are so grateful and thankful that you have allowed us to spend time with you over the last ten years.

On a personal note, I would like to thank my Burrrr and the four CJs who continue to teach me about love and laughter every single day.

And finally, in the immortal words of our beloved General George Hammond, "Good luck and God speed."

Christopher Judge
Vancouver, August 2007

Full Circle

Just another everyday mission to save the galaxy.
Indeed.

And so, all good things must come to an end. Well... sort of. After a record breaking ten-year journey, *Stargate SG-1* finishes its momentous run on the Sci Fi network in its present television incarnation – a decade after the inaugural episode, 'Children of the Gods', aired in 1997. Yet whilst season ten has finally been wrapped up, it by no means precedes the end of the *Stargate* franchise, nor does it signify the break-up of the SG-1 team. Taken back to the big screen, and with a new spin-off series, *Stargate SG-1* seems to have come full circle – it's the end of a chapter, but the beginning of a new story.

"Not many people get to say they've worked on a show for ten years," smiles *Stargate SG-1*'s executive producer, Brad Wright, proudly. Having co-created the hit television show with Jonathan Glassner, Wright has fair reason to be proud. With a record breaking 214 episodes, *Stargate SG-1* is officially the longest consecutive-running science fiction show of all time, securing a well-deserved spot in the *Guinness World Records* book.

"It probably won't happen again in my career, I doubt it will happen in any of our careers again," Wright continues. "It's a rare and unusual thing that was born out of unusual circumstances – one of which was the fact that we were first aired on Showtime for five years and then the second five years was spent on the Sci Fi Channel. We were allowed two lives."

As a series, *Stargate SG-1* certainly has legs, and it's no wonder that hundreds of episodes later, there are still more stories to tell. The Stargate itself is the perfect storytelling device in science fiction – creating endless possibilities and scenarios. Combining and deconstructing a fistful of genres: science fiction, supernatural horror, social satire, romance, action-adventure and comedy – and all served up with witty dialogue and kick-ass action, *Stargate SG-1*'s decade-long run made the show an international hit, overtaking such phenomena as *The X-Files* and *Star Trek*.

Yet, every year since season six, the show's writers planned the series finale. Expecting the plug to be pulled on their show, they made sure that the final

Opposite: Vala Mal Doran (Claudia Black), blending in with the Ori.
Below: Cameron Mitchell (Ben Browder) reflects on his time leading the SG-1 team.

Full Circle

Above: *The Ori's frontwoman, Adria (Morena Baccarin), is SG-1's most powerful adversary to date.*

episode of seasons six, seven, eight and nine, tied up any loose ends. For the first time in years, the writers, producers, crew and cast members all believed that there would be another season. The actors had signed a contract for season eleven, and creatively, the show had a lot more to offer. Ironically, this confidence seemed to be the kiss of death.

"In terms of looking back over the stories, they were some of the strongest stories we've done in a while," says writer Joe Mallozzi, who has been a key member of the renowned writing team since season four. "Every season has its hits and misses, but I think season ten had far more hits than maybe previous years."

"For me, it was kind of ironic that it was our last season," adds Paul Mullie, who makes up the other half of Mallozzi's writing partnership. "It didn't feel like it was our last season, and for once we didn't really wrap up the show – which is what we'd been doing for years. We didn't do that this year, and in a way, that was kind of ironic. Although I'm not bitter about the cancellation of the show, because ten seasons is an amazing accomplishment for everyone involved, I still think the show could have kept going. Creatively, the basic idea is so open-ended that there's no limit to where you can go with that basic concept. I think those characters were still working well together, and they still had their basic issues to work out. For me, it was kind of funny that season ten was our last season because it just felt like a good, solid, middle of the run season. It could have just kept on going."

And millions of fans worldwide agreed. Without ever straying from its basic story and characters, *Stargate SG-1* could swing from outright science fiction to comedy to heartbreaking family drama. Over the years, it touched upon many of life's toughest issues: separation,

Above: Teal'c (Christopher Judge) prepares for SG-1's toughest battle yet.

rejection, the death of a loved one, the alienation of old friends and facing the loss of new ones. Season ten, perhaps more than ever, brought many moral questions to light – good people can do bad things, bad people can do good things, and beloved characters can die. And more often than not, these deaths cannot be reversed by the wonders that come with science fiction.

"I really took a personal interest in season nine, in terms of the new cast, reinventing the show, and new bad guys the Ori," shares executive producer Robert C. Cooper. "I just found that we had barely begun telling those stories in season nine, so season ten was when we really got into the meat of it. Season nine was more talking about the bad guys coming. Season ten was when the battle got going. I also think that season nine was kind of like season one of a new show and so sometimes it takes you a little while to find your feet. Ben [Browder] got more comfortable in season ten and I really enjoyed the cast's chemistry that gelled early on in season nine, but really found its form in season ten. It was funny because for so long, we always felt that four was the magic number on how many people could be on the team. Five always seemed like an odd number and we weren't sure it would work – it turns out it does."

If five became the show's new magic number, it had a lot to do with · *Stargate SG-1's* newest cast member. With the addition of Claudia Black as a fully-fledged series regular, season ten was injected with genuine humor, romantic chemistry, and a fantastic spin on the fledgling Ori story arc.

Claudia Black's real-life pregnancy fed into the plot, with her giving birth to a miracle child who becomes the powerful leader of the Ori. It is this first episode, 'Flesh and Blood', which marks the prevalent story arc for the final season, and shows that Vala more than deserves a place in the SG-1 team, and Claudia in *Stargate SG-1*.

Full Circle

"Vala brings a liveliness and a spunk to *Stargate SG-1*," explains Cooper. "She's kind of a walking 'id'. She gets to say things that other people wouldn't say and she has a playfulness and an attitude that doesn't really come out in the show, because the characters are military for the most part and they are confined by those restrictions. Daniel Jackson tends to be a very sincere character, and of course Teal'c is not wacky by any means, so to have a character who is inherently more free and fun just adds an extra dimension to the team."

Black's witty banter and levity certainly adds a comedic dimension to the show, but she combines this with the ability to play the serious storylines with grave sincerity, in a wonderful dichotomy of weighty drama and gut-busting humor.

As a renegade alien, it is Vala who advises the SG-1 team on many other-world matters, allowing them into her world, as much as they have allowed her into theirs. Her wide-eyed, matter-of-fact delivery of her lines, whether they concern teasing her fellow team-mates, or affairs of the heart, brings out the jocoseness of her observations, all of which come from a different, "non-human" perspective.

"It felt like Vala was a big part of season nine, because she was in the first six episodes as well as the last episode, so she had a significant presence," explains Wright. "It's funny because there are characters

whose voice you have a difficult time finding as a writer, and there are characters who you just feel like you know right away, and for me, Vala was easy to write. I had fun with her character and she makes a fairly indelible mark. Claudia was a wonderful addition to the cast."

But Vala wasn't to be the only addition to the cast. Pregnant at the end of season nine, the show's writers wanted to come up with a way of integrating her expanding waistline into the story.

"Claudia got pregnant, so it was like, 'Eh... Okay... how are we going to work this in?'" laughs Mullie. "Then it was like, 'Alright, she's having the child of the Ori.' There were some people who were worried about parallels to certain religions, but we decided not to worry too much about that. It was just kind of an obvious way to deal with her pregnancy really, and then when it came time to cast the part of Adria, we had to buy that she was Vala's daughter to a certain extent. I think Morena Baccarin fits the bill. I think it worked out pretty well."

Giving the Ori a beautiful face, Baccarin was more than happy to step into the role of Adria. Named after Vala's evil stepmother, Adria, a genetically advanced human infused with Ori knowledge, was created to circumvent the rule that the Ori cannot directly use their powers to conquer the Milky Way Galaxy. The fact that she is human is made evident by her lingering affections for her mother.

Above: Judge and Browder, being a lot more welcoming to Cliff Simon off-screen that their alter egos are to Ba'al.

Full Circle

Above: *Look up!*
The quest for the
Sangraal continues...

"I have to give Robert credit for that whole arc," says Wright. "We spun various scenarios, but I think he was afraid to propose the virgin birth scenario for all of its implications and how it might be construed. The fact is that it went well with the mythology that the Ori would try to sneak one by us and breach the rules of the Ancients in our galaxy and basically send one of their own. The fact that there's a familiar relationship with Vala just makes it more believable and honest."

"We needed a bad guy," adds Cooper. "The Ori were a faceless idea and to have a person that we could identify that we were squaring off against was important. Morena did a great job of being that force to be reckoned with."

Known for her role as Inara Serra in Joss Whedon's short-lived series *Firefly*, Morena Baccarin was cast to play the adult version of Adria, appearing in five episodes of the last season – though her presence was felt throughout. Sired by the Ori to lead their bloody crusade on Earth, Adria was season ten's 'big bad' who grew into a full-grown woman with overwhelming powers in a matter of weeks. Throughout the season, SG-1 had to struggle against their most powerful foe yet, who nonetheless harbors strong affection towards Vala, hoping to convert her to a belief in the Ori.

This brought about a darker theme in the series, one which allowed it to be debated by academics as well as enjoyed by millions of the show's core fan base. The metaphor of the Ori as religious fanatics is certainly a popular discussion point this season. A logical progression, the Ori follow traditional *Stargate* themes of false gods and power-hungry rulers

who are willing to kill those who go against their beliefs. Philosophically, it's a very interesting moral argument.

"I just felt like we had always had a rich tradition of dealing with religions, false religions and beliefs on the show that was built into the mythology and I wanted to find a way to make the show a little more current and a little more poignant in terms of what we are going through in our own day to day lives," explains Cooper thoughtfully. "As a writer, you always want to speak through your writing. Not that we were overly heavy handed – you want to entertain people. I'm not interested in preaching. But I do think it's important that science fiction has relatable dramatic elements to it so that people will enjoy it. Relatable characters and relatable stories are what make people enjoy the show as viewers. I wanted to speak to certain ideas that I think were around me at the time. I think all of us as writers want to be able to take things from our lives and put them in our writing. That's what makes it a little bit real. When you have philosophical arguments with various religious people, the whole challenge is how do you prove whose god exists or whether god exists at all?"

The science versus faith debate is certainly an innate undercurrent of the season, if not the whole series. In 'Line in the Sand', Carter states her

Above: *Old friends reunite – just ignore the puppeteer!*

Full Circle

Above: The original trio follow "invisible" O'Neill in '200'. belief in God – showing that science and faith are not necessarily mutually exclusive. The introduction of Adria shows the adverse affects of having faith without doubt, and her unfaltering devotion to the Book of Origin only secures her comparison with organised religious followers.

But, sadly for SG-1, Adria is not the only villain the team find themselves battling this year. As of season ten, Ba'al becomes the longest-lasting Goa'uld in the series and the longest-running villain of the show. Yet, in a wonderful twist of fate, it is he who brings about the death of Adria in an attempt to manipulate her powers over the Ori army. The penultimate episode, 'Dominion', sees the marriage of old villains with new ones – the Goa'uld versus the Ori. Ba'al's takeover of Adria has been nicknamed "Baadria" by the fans, and is a fitting culmation of a season that has seen SG-1 face an enormity of evil.

This season, SG-1 has seen an assortment of quirky and audacious characters, many of whom would easily serve as the nucleus of a future series. Fans who have been with the characters since the beginning have grown to love the expanding cast, the intricate season-long storylines and the scripts that constantly keep you guessing.

"The thing about *Stargate SG-1* is that if you look across the ten seasons of the show, you're going to see a gradual but significant evolutionary change in how the show, as well as the characters, developed," Wright explains. "It's because of the input of our writing staff, who have managed to stick together for a very long time, and Robert's hand in seasons nine and ten of the show. But also the performers – how they grow as actors and characters and how they become richer people onscreen. If you go back, for example, and look at Daniel in season one, he was great, but he was doing Daniel as James Spader from the movie, and now in season ten there's a rich, thoughtful and wiser character that comes not just from Michael's experience of ten years as a performer, but Daniel's experience as someone who's traveled through the gate for ten years.

Above: *Harriman (Gary Jones) does what he does best.*

"Our universe expanded this season in terms of our capability significantly. I had always resisted technology so easily being turned around and used. In seasons two and three of *Stargate SG-1*, I didn't want us to have ships and ray guns because that just made us another science fiction show. What makes *Stargate* unique is the people from the here-and-now going forward, but it's been so long, we've been going through the Stargate for so long over the series, that it's inevitable that we'd learn new technology and start building our own stuff. So we had the *Odyssey*, we had the *Daedalus*, the *Prometheus* has come and gone we're so far along, and that has made it a more significant and potent potion in the *Stargate* universe. We've beaten a lot of bad guys. We've defeated the Goa'uld and that's changed the way of the galaxy. I'd say that, creatively, those are fairly big differences. The humanity that *Stargate SG-1* represents in terms of Earth is a much more potent force than when we first ventured forward with our fans onboard."

Stargate SG-1's fan base is unusually zealous. Television writers usually toil in anonymity, but *Stargate* fans know who wrote and directed every episode. Every cult show since *Star Trek* has had a write-in campaign of some sort, designed to save it from the TV junk heap. Usually it's a small but vocal bunch of die-hards who want to rescue a show that was axed due to sagging ratings. But since *Stargate SG-1's* cancellation was announced, viewers around the world have been trying to show that the Sci Fi Channel has let down its biggest group of fans yet.

The cancellation came on the heels of *Stargate SG-1's* two hundredth episode (a huge milestone for the cast and crew alike), and the news soon leaked out that the announcement came at the party celebrating that seminal episode. But whilst the series has had some sort of closure, it has certainly not ended.

"Ultimately, at the end of the day (in my mind) the stories just keep going," shares Mullie. "The characters are still out there. Yes, they're doing movies, but I mean creatively, how I think about the show, I think about it as an open ended concept. I like that season ten wasn't a big wrap-up season in that sense. Robert very deliberately wrote the last episode that way – he called it 'Unending' for a reason. I think that was a great way to go out. Ten seasons in, we were still introducing new elements, which shows that the series is still alive. We weren't limping towards the finish line at all."

Creatively, part of what makes the show special is not only the continuity of the cast in front of the camera, but also the people behind it. So what explanation does Brad Wright – a man who has been behind the well-oiled *Stargate* machine since day one – have for the show's successful longevity?

"We've been around for such a long time because of a combination of different aspects," answers Wright easily. "First, the cast is always number one. People don't watch television to just follow a story (although that is very important), they watch to follow characters, and they are very interested and they are very invested in the characters of *Stargate SG-1*. Secondly, I would say that *Stargate SG-1* takes place in the here-and-now, and not in the distant future – which is another way of doing science fiction. Thirdly, I would say that the series has always maintained a sense of humor. To say that we don't take ourselves very seriously is an understatement. I just surround myself with very funny writers and we enjoy humor and that's the way it translates on the screen. And finally, I would say continuity of talent behind the scenes. Quite often a show will die because the people who originally brought it to you have moved on, and new people come in and they'll want to brand it with their own vision, therefore it changes in a radical way and that disenfranchises the audience. I think our audience has stuck with us because we've stuck with it. Robert and I have been around since the beginning, Paul and Joe have been around since season four – that's a long time for television writers to stick with a series. That's why I'm surprised we lasted so long. The cast and crew have all stuck with it, so I'm surprised... but very happy." Å

Opposite: The cast give everyone a round of applause at the end of shooting Stargate SG-1's final episode.

"Unfortunately, right now, there is no war. In a war, you have two sides fighting. All we have is a lot of winning by the bad guys."

EXECUTIVE PRODUCERS:
Robert C. Cooper & Brad Wright

REGULAR CAST:
Michael Shanks as Dr Daniel Jackson
Ben Browder as Lieutenant Colonel Cameron Mitchell
Amanda Tapping as Lieutenant Colonel Samantha Carter
Christopher Judge as Teal'c
Beau Bridges as Major General Hank Landry
Claudia Black as Vala Mal Doran

RECURRING SPECIAL GUEST STARS AND RECURRING CAST:
Morena Baccarin as Adria (7, 10, 11, 14, 19)
Cliff Simon as Ba'al (4, 10, 11, 19)
Eric Breker as Colonel Reynolds (5, 12, 17, 19)
Martin Christopher as Major Marks (1, 7, 9, 18, 20)
Bill Dow as Dr Bill Lee (4, 13, 15, 18)
Matthew Glave as Colonel Paul Emerson (1, 3, 7, 9)
Gary Jones as Chief Master Sergeant Walter Harriman (1, 3, 4, 6-9, 15, 17, 18, 20)

Flesh and Blood

Written by: Robert C. Cooper Directed by: William Waring	Guest Cast: Doug Abrahams (Prior), Tony Amendola (Bra'tac), Garry Chalk (Colonel Chekov), Emma Rose (Adria at age 4), Jodelle Ferland (Adria at age 7), Tim Guinee (Tomin), Gwenda Lorenzetti (Nursemaid), Brenna O'Brien (Adria at age 12), Robert Picardo (Richard Woolsey), Eric Steinberg (Netan), Apollonia Vanova (Russian Weapons Officer), Bruno Verdoni (Netan's Lieutenant)

Having become pregnant in the Ori's home galaxy, the season ten premiere sees Vala Mal Doran give birth to her child – a baby girl who is immediately taken away and proclaimed to be Orici by a Prior. He declares that she belongs to those who follow the path and will lead them to victory over the non-believers. Meanwhile, Samantha Carter remains suspended in space, drifting over the Supergate, eventually managing to make contact with Lieutenant Colonel Cameron Mitchell, who had lost consciousness when the *Korolev* exploded. Docking the *Odyssey*, Mitchell attempts to beam Carter aboard, but the badly damaged craft has not recovered its beaming capacity. With only a couple of hours of life-support left, Carter can only wait… The team is scattered – Daniel Jackson's whereabouts are unknown and Teal'c is taken captive onboard a Lucian Alliance vessel. Netan, leader of the Lucian Alliance ship, believes that SG-1 intentionally dragged them into battle knowing it would deplete their forces. He orders them to surrender the *Odyssey* or be destroyed. On the Ori ship, Vala is permitted to see her daughter, who is rapidly growing and is now four years old. She insists that she will help her mother find the path of the Ori. With the teleporters still off-line and Sam's air running out, Mitchell takes the controls of the *Odyssey* and picks Sam up directly. He reveals that someone used the teleport rings to get off the *Korolev*, and they hope it was Jackson. Indeed, the *Korolev* was hit, and Jackson beamed off the ship and onto the Ori vessel – where he locates Vala. Daniel and Vala plan to capture Adria and turn her against the Ori, but Tomin captures Daniel instead. Daniel stuns Tomin and he and Vala are beamed aboard the *Odyssey*. As SG-1 regroup, Mitchell declares that they need a plan… and a damn good one at that.

Prior: With the wisdom of the ages, she will lead us to glorious victory over any and all unbelievers.

"When you write the first episode of a new season, oftentimes it's just a question of putting the pieces back together after the cliffhanger from the year before – and there was quite a spectacular mess made by the loose ends at the conclusion of 'Camelot'," shares 'Flesh and Blood' writer Robert Cooper.

Above: Mitchell has his work cut out for him in season ten.

The season nine finale, 'Camelot', leaves Carter drifting in space, Ori ships coming through the Supergate, and a heavily pregnant Vala in labor. Having been on the losing end of a major battle, the season ten premiere was about introducing Adria as the new bad guy as well as seeing SG-1 get back on their feet. "We got our asses kicked last season, so now we need to get back in the race," says Cooper. "I really like the sequence when Carter is stuck in a spacesuit out in space. That, drowning and being buried alive are just horrible, horrible scenarios that make your heart beat faster and you get a little bit breathless even just thinking about being in that situation. It's a great dramatic situation to put Carter in."

But Carter was not the only character in a dramatic situation. Marking Claudia Black's first appearance as a series regular, 'Flesh and Blood' kicks off a major story arc of season ten – the battle against the Ori. It's within this arc that Black's Vala Mal Doran plays a pivotal role as the mother of new villain Adria. Created to cheat the ascended rules of non-intervention, Adria is essentially an Ori in human form, known as an Orici.

"It was really interesting to have the mother-daughter relationship between Vala and Adria," shares Cooper. "I think that was the key in making it interesting and believable that Vala would become part of the SG-1 team. She was such an independent character, not the sort that SG-1 would normally trust, so we needed some reason why she would join up and why we would let her join up. The fact that Adria is her daughter gave us a connection."

Rapidly growing from birth, Adria at different ages was played by different actresses in the episode, the youngest of whom was played by Robert Cooper's daughter, Emma Rose.

"It wasn't something we sought out, it was more of a functional thing," explains Cooper. "The girl we hired to play the role froze up on set and couldn't go through with it. I knew my daughter would fit the wardrobe and that she might be able to pull it off. It turned out to be a pretty good experience for her. If you talk about the experience, she's very proud of it because it was a challenge for her, but it's not something that is ever-present in her mind – she's five, so it's really more what's in front of her at the moment."

Vala: Well, she started off all sweet and innocent, and now she's hell-bent on domination of the galaxy.
Daniel: What? How old is she?
Vala: A few hours.

Finding a range of girls who looked similar enough to play the same character wasn't an easy task. The trick, according to Cooper? Hats.

"The first Adria aside, the two other girls who played Adria in the middle age and the older age were brilliant. When I first turned the script in, the other writers said, 'You're crazy, you're never going to find actors that could possibly be related or look even reasonably similar.' The trick to that is a hat. The more you physically put on the character, the more you believe it's the same face even though their faces weren't that similar. We had to pick sets of girls who looked similar to each other and to Vala. We could have explained it away saying that it's the Ori child, but it certainly looks better if they have a tinge of Vala in them."

The challenge of finding a last-minute replacement is something that may arise when casting young children. "It's difficult because the first Adria didn't work out so well," adds director Will Waring. "In casting, everything went

fine, but on the set there's a hundred grips and electrics standing around, things go a different path sometimes, but in the end it all worked out."

For Waring, who has been working on *Stargate SG-1* since the pilot episode – albeit as a cameraman at first – getting the chance to direct season ten's first episode was an exciting challenge.

"'Flesh and Blood' was a lot of fun," enthuses Waring. "It was chock-a-block full with all kinds of great stuff. We had Carter floating in space and Mitchell escaping the exploding hangar bay. For the fireball scene, we were using figures in place of the actors. After the first take, Ben Browder said, 'I think I can get a little closer to it,' and I was like, 'I don't think you should. It's very hot!' As we're rolling, he runs out, then stops for a bit, hangs out, looks around and then runs with this fireball right at his ass! He was like, 'See, I told you I could get a little closer!' It looks fantastic!"

Another particularly memorable aspect of 'Flesh and Blood' for both Waring and the show's viewers was the grand Ori ship set which allowed us a glimpse into the enemy's vessel.

"The Ori ship was great!" recalls the director. "They did a fantastic job lighting it, and they did an incredible job building it – especially considering it was done so quickly. It looked fantastic and it was a real flat-out design. I remember when I got to set, there weren't that many hallways built yet, so we had to make two hallways look like every different hallway in that episode. So that was certainly interesting!" Å

Above: Daniel Jackson (Michael Shanks) comes to rescue Vala from her newborn daughter.

Morpheus

Written by: Joseph Mallozzi & Paul Mullie Directed by: Andy Mikita	Guest Cast: Toby Berner (Grimsby), Chris Bradford (Medical Technician), Patrick Gilmore (Ackerman), Robin Mossley (Dr Reimer), Robert Picardo (Richard Woolsey), Benjamin Ratner (Dr Hutchison)

Six worlds have fallen to the Ori in eight days. In an attempt to find the Ancient weapon, SG-1 gate to Vagonbrei – one of the planets Arthur and his knights went to in their quest for the Holy Grail. Vala stays behind as she needs to pass a psych evaluation before she is cleared for off-world travel. SG-1 find Vagonbrei abandoned and full of skeletons. Most of the villagers have died in their beds. Daniel discovers that, according to legend, a cave overlooking the village was once home to Morgan Le Fay – King Arthur's half-sister and an adversary of Merlin. She may have taken the weapon they seek from Merlin. Back at SGC, Vala gets increasingly nervous about her evaluation, and thinks that she can rehearse her answers. Her planned responses are met with frustration. On Vagonbrei, SG-1 find Ackerman sleeping and can't rouse him. The team's bloodwork shows an elevated white cell count and a marked increase in serotonin levels. Whatever has affected Ackerman has infected them too. They must stay awake as long as possible – if they fall asleep, they may never wake up. At SGC, Woolsey tells Vala that he can make sure she passes her evaluation in return for insight into the weekly goings-on at Stargate Command. She rejects his offer. Dr Reimer discovers a dormant parasite in a soil sample which reacts when it comes into contact with live tissue. The parasite gorges on melatonin, finally provoking a lethal aneurysm. Mitchell and Teal'c find a lizard which must be immune to the mysterious affliction as it is still active – if they can catch it, they can reverse-engineer an antidote. Teal'c captures the lizard but the team collapses from exhaustion. A hazmat team retrieves SG-1 and takes them back to SGC where they are cured. Vala passes her psychiatric evaluation, as Woolsey's offer was part of a test to make sure she could be trusted – and a well-rested Daniel reveals that he found a reference in the Vagonbrei library to Atlantis…

Mitchell: This place is deader than a Texas salad bar.

Named after the Greek god of dreams, 'Morpheus' is in part an episode about people falling asleep – and this generated concern from the network, who thought it would fail to keep the viewers awake. But what

they hadn't foreseen was Claudia Black's terrific portrayal of former Goa'uld host turned psych experiment Vala Mal Doran.

Above: Vala makes sure the viewers stay awake in 'Morpheus'.

"She's just a lot of fun to write for," shares executive producer Joe Mallozzi. "You know when you give Claudia humor, she'll deliver, and she certainly did. You don't want to make the show boring, you don't want the audience to fall asleep. That's why it was nice to cut between the serious A-story and the punchier B-story as well."

A standalone episode, 'Morpheus', apart from anything else, gave viewers an insight in to why Vala would want to join Stargate Command... and more importantly, why they would accept her. Surely SG-1 weren't just going to offer a notorious thief and con-artist a position on the team?

For writer and executive producer Paul Mullie, the answer was a resounding, "No".

"It doesn't make sense for her to be accepted as an alien," he explains, "and not a very trustworthy alien at that point, either, so we knew she would have to go through some hoops. We liked the idea of the psychological evaluation."

In fact, the idea of the evaluation came from Claudia Black herself, who knew her roguish, dishonest character would have to prove her worth to the team. "When we came up with the premise of 'Morpheus', it was purely a standalone episode," says Mallozzi. "But after talking to the other writers, we decided to tie it in with the quest for the Sangraal, and that's why they go to the planet and they get into trouble. We had always intended for Vala to join the team, so when Claudia came to us with this idea, we thought it was a great way to analyze her character and make the episode more fun."

For director Andy Mikita, the juxtaposition of the impending danger SG-1 faced on Vagonbrei with Vala's light-hearted B-story broke up the pace of the episode, allowing the viewer to step back and take a breath. "That was a lot of fun," he recalls. "Ben Ratner, who played Dr Hutchison, is a very well-known Vancouver actor, he's done a ton of stuff and he's a very talented guy. I thought those scenes with him and Vala were wonderful. I really wanted to get my hands on an old-fashioned lie detector with the arm that would squiggle back and forth for the tests he did on Vala. It looked like we weren't going to be able to get one, but then Kenny Gibbs, our prop master, found one and I was really excited! The guy who was operating the machine was actually from the police department, and it was a real machine. It wasn't something that had been rigged up especially for film use, and he was trying to get it to do all this stuff for us and was like, 'Oh, that's not how these machines are supposed to work – they're not supposed to do that.' We were like, 'That doesn't matter – make the arms go back and forth really fast – who cares?' We all tried it out, of course. The guy actually gave us little secrets about how to cheat the machine," Mikita laughs. "Obviously, I can't disclose any of that information under punishment of death – he knows where I live!"

Landry: Well, you can't cram for a psychiatric evaluation.
Vala: That's what they want you to think.

A further challenge for the director, and what made 'Morpheus' so memorable, was in conveying the eerie atmosphere of Vagonbrei – an abandoned town infected with a sleep-inducing parasite. Visually, 'Morpheus' is unlike any other *Stargate SG-1* episode. Nervous about the network's initial comments on the episode, Mikita was determined to prove them wrong. "A large problem of that episode revolved around our village set, which we had built a couple of seasons before," shares Mikita.

"Because of the cost of building such a vast set, we had to amortize the cost of that by shooting in there as often as possible – trying to make it look as different as possible every time we would go in. One of the things that myself, cinematographer Peter Woeste and designer James Robbins talked about doing was making it feel like a deserted town. We covered it with vines and we shot everything very black-and-white – we took a lot of color out, used a lot of smoke and shot it later in the day as opposed to having the sun appearing. We wanted it to have a cool, dank feel to it with a spooky vibe, and I think it worked."

Above: Sleeping on the job? Sam Carter (Amanda Tapping) and Daniel are saved just in time.

Mikita isn't the only one to enjoy the aesthetics of 'Morpheus'. Mallozzi was equally pleased with the final product. "Andy did a great job directing the episode, creating that creepy, sleepy atmosphere, and it was actually my favorite episode from season ten. We always enjoy writing these standalone stories because they're so hard to do. Frankly, after nine-plus years of television, and all the sci-fi that has come before us, it's very easy to just focus on the arc-driven stories. I'm not saying they're easy to write, but they are easier than coming up with an episode where the team goes off-world, deals with an issue and then comes back. 'Morpheus' was very well directed and it was one of those episodes where everything came together nicely." Å

The Pegasus Project

Written by: Brad Wright Directed by: William Waring	Guest Cast: Joe Flanigan (Lieutenant Colonel John Sheppard), David Hewlett (Dr Rodney McKay), Torri Higginson (Dr Elizabeth Weir), Chelah Horsdal (Lieutenant Womack), David Nykl (Dr Radek Zelenka) Sarah Strange (Morgan Le Fay), Matthew Walker (Merlin), Chuck Campbell (Technician)

Continuing their search for the Ancient weapon, SG-1 heads to Atlantis in the hope of preventing the Ori from getting more ships through the Supergate. They intend to move a second Stargate near the Ori Supergate and supply a huge burst of energy from nuclear bombs to force the gate to jump and link it to a black hole to force the Supergate to remain open, preventing the Ori from creating a new wormhole. Remaining at Atlantis to look for information on Merlin's weapon, Daniel and Vala accompany Dr Elizabeth Weir to the virtual reality room to question a holographic interface who takes the form of a Lantian woman. Daniel is suspicious of the hologram, and discovers it is in fact Morgan Le Fay. Aboard the *Odyssey*, the first warhead is launched, but is unsuccessful. McKay discovers that they need to use two bombs, but the second attempt is also unsuccessful, though energy does pass between the Stargate and the Supergate. They have two bombs left. McKay wants to increase the yield to maximum and try again – but a maximum yield could vaporize both gates. The *Odyssey* is attacked by the Wraith, but Carter beams two nuclear bombs onto the hive ship, eliminating not only the Wraith ship, but sealing off the gate to the Ori ships and destroying one in the process. Back on Atlantis, Morgan Le Fay reveals herself to be an ascended Ancient and is close to breaking her vow of non-interference to help SG-1 in their battle against the Ori. As she begins to tell Daniel and Vala what planet to go to, she is cut off and disappears – it's now clearer than ever that they're in this battle alone.

Mitchell: This place is Daniel Disneyland.

The task, or rather the honor, of penning the first *Stargate SG-1* and *Stargate: Atlantis* major crossover episode fell to executive producer Brad Wright. With *Stargate: Atlantis* being picked up for its fourth season, Wright no longer felt the need to keep the two shows entirely separate – so, with this in mind, he took an incredibly excited Daniel to the lost city

of Atlantis.

Above: Daniel *finally gets to Atlantis.*

"As much as I enjoyed 'The Pegasus Project' personally because it was fun to do, it was weird to do it in Atlantis," grins Wright. "I kept forgetting what series I was writing for – it's a bit of a jigsaw puzzle of both shows. In this business you do a lot of writing whether your name is going to be on a script or not. But when your name is going to be on it you want it to be special."

According to the ratings, 'The Pegasus Project' was very special indeed. A big fan favorite, the episode not only took Daniel to his long-time dream destination, but more importantly, it gave SG-1 something they desperately needed... it gave them a win.

"The fans really liked this episode and I don't think it's just because it's a crossover," explains Wright. "We delivered quite a lot of the things people like to see in an episode of *Stargate SG-1*. People in our audience love to see our team win, and it had been quite some time since we had won. They didn't just win a little bit, they won big, and through a ton of circumstances which I stumbled into rather than cleverly plotted at the beginning," he laughs. "The original idea was to use the explosion of the Wraith ship to provide the power to make the gate jump to the Supergate and create a continuously open Stargate that would close the Supergate to the Ori for some time. But I thought, 'Well, if there's an Ori ship in the area, maybe a kawoosh of the Supergate could overcome the shield and we could at least get rid of one of those big ships. It's the ultimate 'two birds with one stone' scenario. The goal was to connect the Supergates, and in one big swoop all of a sudden our guys get rid of two of the armies at the same time. That was fun, I think our audience enjoyed it, and they didn't see it coming, which is always the hard part. Our fans are so savvy because they know the show, they know the characters, and they often think they know where we're going. Often they're right, and they like knowing they're right, but I think I pulled a few along the way."

Sheppard: Listen, if McKay gives you a hard time, just...
Mitchell: Shoot him.
Sheppard: Also he's mortally allergic to citrus.
Mitchell: Really?
Sheppard: [Pulls out a lemon] Keep one with me at all times. Just a comfort to know it's there.

For Wright, 'The Pegasus Project' also provided some rationale to Daniel's failed ascension. The archaeologist was sent back to mortality after breaking the rule of non-interference in the season seven episode 'Full Circle'.

"I wanted Daniel to get mad at the Ancients," reveals Wright. "'Get off your ass! Do something!' Daniel was cast away because he didn't fit in, he wasn't going to not interfere – not when humanity was at stake. The original notion of 'The Pegasus Project' was a Daniel story – that's where my idea came from. I wanted Daniel to go to the computer and have it be a real Ancient. I thought that was kind of a neat twist. The other storyline with the gate came up when I was working out something for the rest of the team to do and it turned out to be fun and exciting for them, too."

An impressive episode in terms of visual effects, Wright explains that one of the biggest challenges of 'The Pegasus Project' was the shooting schedule.

"It could have used a little more action," he says candidly. "I wish we'd had another day to shoot it, but when you're spending so much money on visual effects, there's just no way we could do that. The thing that people have to realize is that if they have criticisms about this

show – what we did or didn't do – we have finite financial resources. We'd love to do the bigger version, we'd love to, but we can't because we don't have the money. Quite often we sacrifice one episode financially, make it a smaller story, so we can bolster another. That's the tightrope walk of being a producer."

For director Will Waring, the crossover was a new opportunity to go to the *Stargate: Atlantis* set and shoot, direct and work with the show's actors.

"It was great to get to go over to the other set. I remember before we did the briefing room scene in Atlantis, the room was being prepped and they put little place cards on the table, like setting up a big dinner. We were like, 'Joe here, Amanda there… no, let's move these around and put Joe here, no – let's put Joe between Claudia and Amanda. That'll work nicely.' So that was a lot of fun. You get a great interaction between the SG-1 group and the Atlantis group. One of my favorite scenes is on the bridge of the *Odyssey* when they are flying into Atlantis – the look on Daniel's face is great. This is where he's wanted to be for such a long time. It's just a shame he spent all his time in the library," jokes Waring, who on reflection, says that 'The Pegasus Project' is his favorite episode of the season.

"Every episode has a bunch of scenes in it that I just love to death," points out the director. "But if I had to pick one as my favorite from beginning to end, it would be 'Pegasus Project'. The fact that you've got the two groups together creates a great dynamic, and I just like the idea that Daniel gets to go where he's always wanted to go for so many years. I think that's a really nice payoff." Å

Insiders

| Written by: Alan McCullough | Guest Cast: Dan Shea (Sergeant Siler), Peter Flemming |
| Directed by: Peter F. Woeste | (NID Agent Barrett), Lesley Ewen (SGC Geneticist), Paul Christie (Caffey) |

With Daniel searching for further information on Merlin's weapon in Camelot's library, the rest of SG-1 meet with Landry to discuss the results of their *Pegasus* expedition. But they are interrupted by the arrival of an Al'kesh bomber heading straight for Cheyenne Mountain. The vessel is disabled and it crash-lands – whereupon SG-1 discover the pilot is none other than the Goa'uld Ba'al. Taking him back to the SGC, Sam detects that Ba'al has implanted himself with a locator beacon. He refuses to speak to anyone except SG-1, and tells them that his clones want him dead. He needs their help to get rid of the clones and promises that in return he will give them valuable information that will aid them in their search for Merlin's weapon. Ba'al tells them that he has implanted a locator chip in every one of his clones, and in himself to gain the clones' trust. SG-1 are skeptical, but they decide to investigate, and Vala is allowed to go on her first off-world mission. Tracking the clones to different planets, SG-1 take another Ba'al prisoner – he, too, claims to be the 'real' Ba'al who knows where the weapon is. When the team returns to Stargate Command with two Ba'als, they find out that SG-12 has also brought in two clones, as did SG-14. Unauthorized to talk to the Ba'als, Agent Barrett of the NID disobeys Landry's orders and enters one of the holding rooms. His gun is taken by a Ba'al, who frees the other Ba'als and uses stolen zat guns to knock out Sam and Barrett. Carter is threatened with Barrett's life to download the list of planets from the Ancient database, as the Ba'als want Merlin's weapon for themselves. Once they have the information, the Ba'als beam onto a waiting Al'kesh. Together, the locator beacons in the clones combines to amplify a signal, enough to be picked up through SGC's jamming screen. It seems Ba'al was playing SG-1 all along.

Ba'al: It's the clones. They want me dead.
Teal'c: That would make all of us.

There may be tens of thousands of Goa'uld ruling across the galaxy, but there's only one Ba'al. Well… there was one Ba'al. Now there's quite a few, much to the despair of SG-1. When writer Alan McCullough handed in the

script for 'Insiders', executive producer Joe Mallozzi said it was his best script to date. And McCullough, who joined the *Stargate SG-1* writing team in season nine, had to agree.

Above: Mitchell makes a run for it.

"To that date, I would say it probably was my best script," says the writer. "Prior to that, I had written some scripts for season nine, some of which didn't exactly turn out that well. I was new to the show, and they weren't my best efforts, but 'Insiders' came together pretty well.

"For my first-ever episode, 'Prototype', I had watched a handful of the shows over the course of the nine years, and when I had worked up a story, Rob Cooper sent me some tapes. My agent called me and said some tapes had arrived from Vancouver that would help me do some research for my episode. I went to pick them up, and it was a box of twenty episodes! So I watched twenty episodes for 'Prototype', and from a variety of different seasons. So I kind of jumped in the deep end for my first episode, and then over the course of season nine and season ten, I've now watched every single episode as well as all the episodes of *Stargate: Atlantis*. It took a couple of months, but when we get in the room and everybody's talking back and forth and you're pitching out new ideas, you don't want to sound like an idiot because they did that episode in season six. You really need to know the show well to be able to pitch and participate in the discussion. I know the show pretty well now, and I'm comfortable with the characters."

Mitchell: Chief, we got a full count: two strikes, three Ba'als.

Having written for Ba'al in season nine's 'Stronghold' and 'Off the Grid', McCullough may be the newest member of the illustrious writing team, but he was no stranger to the wry and duplicitous antagonist. The return of SG-1's old nemesis, Goa'uld System Lord Ba'al, was both a continuation of a past plotline and an introduction of Ba'al to the present Ori story arc. Using the Trust's cloning technology to create numerous clones of himself, the ruthless character has become a bigger threat to SG-1 then ever before.

"Ba'al brings so much to the story and he's very fun to write for," explains McCullough. "'Insiders' addressed the fact that all these clones were out there in the galaxy and paved the way for several more clone stories throughout the year. Sometimes I find some of the characters difficult to write for, but not so much Ba'al. For whatever reason, I was just able to capture his voice quite easily. Often, when you add new characters, it's not so easy. I was very concerned at the start of season ten when Vala came into the show that I wasn't going to be able to capture her voice, because she's a character that's near and dear to the hearts of a lot of the people here. I wasn't positive that I was going to be able to get her on the first attempt, but

Ba'al came much more easily. I don't think it's a matter of male versus female. It depends on the character. I've always felt that I can write for Carter quite well – I've had a few successful Carter episodes. When you find the character in a situation that is new, then it's quite challenging. What's the most difficult is when the characters would be in situations that they'd never been in before and I'm trying to write that, whilst also sticking to the nine years of that character's history. There are going to be people who know that character better – obviously you don't want to go against what the character would be doing."

Above: Vala keeps her eye on the Ba'al.

Before the episode was shot, the Sci Fi Channel once again expressed concern over the original storyline and changes had to be made.

"There were some things that were said by the network regarding the episode and we needed to rewrite several parts of the B-story," explains McCullough. "We had some notes from them that they didn't like the way the B-story had been laid out. The B-story was the search for the mole, in which each individual member of the base was interviewed to determine where the leak had occurred – how did the Trust find out about Ba'al? Ultimately we tossed that B-story and wrote it more from the point of view of Agent Barrett coming into the base to try and interview Ba'al, but he felt like he was being stonewalled by Landry – which, of course, is what happened in the end."

With so many Ba'als bouncing around, it was imperative that the episode was shot in a clear and precise way so as not to confuse the viewers… well, to confuse them as little as possible.

"I think as far as how it turned out on the screen, director Peter Woeste did a great job," says McCullough, "but I know he was tearing his hair out because when you shoot so many scenes over and over and over again, adding in Cliff Simon everywhere, it's very challenging. He was rapidly running out of time. He'd come into my office and shake his fists at me because he couldn't get the days he needed. So some of the scenes may not have had the full coverage that the other ones would have, but all in all, I was pretty happy with that episode." Å

Uninvited

Written by: Damian Kindler
Directed by: William Waring

Guest Cast: James Caldwell (Hunter), Keegan Connor Tracy (Dr Redden), Jodie Graham (SG-25 Leader), Brock Johnson (Hunter), Biski Gugushe (SG-11 Leader), Jason Bryden (Trust Operative), John Murphy (Sheriff Stokes)

General Landry orders SG-1 to join him at General O'Neill's log cabin in the woods to take a break from the pressures of work. Mitchell is the first and only member to arrive at the retreat, as Daniel is in London scouring a private library for information on Merlin and Morgan Le Fay; Teal'c has joined SG-3 on P9J-333 where, during a covert observation mission, they discovered a mysterious beast has been attacking the locals; Carter is awaiting the return of Teal'c and Colonel Reynolds; and as Vala can't yet drive, she too waits at SGC. When Mitchell goes for an early morning run, he comes across a hunter in the woods who is shouting for help – he and his friend were attacked by what they assume to be a bear. Meanwhile, Vala and SG-25 join Teal'c and SG-3 on P9J-333 to investigate the savage killings of the planet's villagers. The beast is taken out by Teal'c's grenade, and is brought back to Earth, where Dr Redden performs an autopsy. She discovers that the creature was a docile herbivore, mutated by a foreign parasite which attaches itself to the stomach lining of its host. When SG-11 return from a covert mission on an Ori-converted planet and report a similar vicious animal attack, SG-1 are shocked to realise that it's not the Ori who are culpable, but themselves. The leech-like parasites slip from world to world whenever the Sodan cloaking device is activated – the device's own radiation providing an inter-dimensional bridge putting the user out of phase with our dimension. Furthermore, back in the woods Mitchell follows a trail of blood to find a wounded Trust operative who has been using a stolen Sodan device in the hope of spying on SG-1, thus explaining the savage monster in the forest. SG-1 join Mitchell and Landry to enter the woods and hunt down the mutant. When it attacks, SG-1 bring it down with firepower. Another beast attacks them, and is gunned down. Returning to the cabin, the triumphant team enjoy a game of poker – and Mitchell admits he's finally beginning to relax...

Opposite: General Landry (Beau Bridges) – not doing 'Brokeback Stargate'.

Landry: We all need to stop for air now and then. We'll burn out! That's the one thing you people don't know how to do, so I'm making it an order.

"That was the first time I'd ever done any kind of creature feature," says the director of 'Uninvited', Will Waring. "That was tough, because we had to do a lot of exterior shooting at night. We had two full scheduled nights for when the monster attacks to be done at the end of it. There's only so many hours of night and we had a lot of work to do. Tim [Atkins], my DP [director of photography], did a great job lighting that, so I could pretty much shoot anything I wanted in any direction at night, which is extremely tough. A big challenge when we do [night] shooting is we've got a curfew, so we can only do gunfire up to a certain time. Anything after that, we've got to cut the gunfire. More than half of the gunfire that you see [in 'Uninvited'] is actually a visual effect because [filming was] close to the local houses. Of course, then they're shooting at nothing, because there's no monster there," adds Waring, regarding the episodes classic science fiction demands on the actors. "They have to go, 'Oh, there's something here, it looks like it's there, let's just follow this big bag, and it's pink!'"

Vala: You'd think there'd at least be a label on the side in bold print that says, "Beware: may cause deadly extra-dimensional radioactive monster-causing creature to appear."

Stargate SG-1's visual effects team, led by supervisor Michelle Comens, were charged with creating the creature that would eventually be blended in during post-production.

"Really it should be easier," Comens laughs, when asked what effect night shooting has on her department. "You're not seeing as much of it and you can hide things more. But it was a bit disappointing. We had a problem technically with the creature – it wasn't exactly how we wanted it to turn out. We were using people that we hadn't really used before. A full CG [computer generated] creature is an ambitious thing to do on a TV series, and then to only use it one time… If it's a recurring character you can put a lot more into a creature. The only other thing that we've had on the show like that was the Asgard, and we've had years to develop that, a lot of trial and error to get it right. But having a furry creature on a television timeframe is a pretty challenging thing. So it maybe wasn't exactly as we wanted it to turn out."

One of the most significant aspects of 'Uninvited' was the chance that it gave for the audience to see Mitchell and Landry interact together outside the confines of the SGC. Though the writers' hope was to create

a team-building episode like the ones that worked so successfully in the show's early years, star Ben Browder confesses that he wasn't particularly sold on the original idea.

Above: *The team enjoy some well-earned relaxation time.*

"I had some arguments with Coop [Robert Cooper] about it. There was just some stuff between Landry and Mitchell... It was more some of the stuff that Mitchell was saying that I thought sounded like a lieutenant, not a colonel. That's an issue that you deal with as you go through. The thing is that I'm old enough to be a colonel. I was just on a Navy submarine and there wasn't anybody on that boat older than me. The captain of the boat, a career Navy guy, was younger than I was and yet, when you're playing a lieutenant colonel, you need to be aware of the status and hierarchy that goes on within the military. Because I'm young and because I have, I guess, a goofy personality, sometimes, to me, it doesn't quite work. So in that sense, as an actor, I think I need help from the script. It's an interesting combination. No matter what the writer writes – and the writer can be absolutely correct – sometimes you're going to have to deal with the baggage of the actor's persona or the actor's appearance. There's the reality, the real colonels and the real majors, and then there's the Hollywood reality, and in the back of my brain, knowing what these guys are [really] like, sometimes you want to get closer to reality than Hollywood tends to get." Å

Written by: Paul Mullie, Joseph Mallozzi, Brad Wright, Carl Binder, Martin Gero, Robert C. Cooper, Alan McCullough **Directed by:** Martin Wood	**Guest Cast:** Peter DeLuise (Wormhole X-Treme! Replacement Actor), Trevor Devall (Voice of Asgard), Shirley Hill (Furling), Jonathan Hill (Furling), Julie Johnson (Young Carter), Jason Coleman (Young Daniel), Barbara Kottmeier (Young Vala), Cory Montieth (Young Mitchell), Anwar Hasan (Young Teal'c), Martin Wood (Wormhole X-Treme! Director), Herbert Duncanson (Douglas Anders), Christian Bocher (Raymond Gunne), Jill Teed (Yolanda Reese), Isaac Hayes (Teal'c P.I. Announcer), Richard Dean Anderson (Major General Jack O'Neill), Don S. Davis (Lieutenant General George Hammond), Willie Garson (Martin Lloyd), Pierre Bernard (Zombie)

Mitchell: Yeah. This is going to be huge. The big 2-0-0.

Martin Lloyd returns to the SGC to ask SG-1 to review his movie script. His television show, *Wormhole X-Treme!*, is being made into a feature film. The team is unenthusiastic, especially Mitchell, who is more interested in making his two hundredth trip through the Stargate, but the Pentagon believes that Martin's film would help keep the Stargate program a secret from the public. As Martin goes through his notes however, the team quickly begin pitching their own ideas for the film. Mitchell puts forward an action-packed zombie movie, but Martin is unconvinced. To make matters worse, his main actor has quit, so Carter suggests making the main character invisible – recalling the time O'Neill was rendered invisible by alien technology. The meeting is interrupted by Landry, who needs to send SG-1 on a mission, but the gate fails to power up, and they go back to their discussion. Martin offers up another story of a Replicator attack, but the team still aren't impressed. Next, Vala tells a story about flying a stolen cargo ship when a solar flare from a nearby star wreaked havoc with her navigation system and she was forced to crash-land on a nearby planet. Her story sounds very familiar and Martin soon realises she is describing *The Wizard of Oz*. But Martin's idea for the end of Act Two isn't much better – it involves Cheyenne Mountain blowing up and the deus ex machina of beaming out the heroes at the last minute. Scene twenty-four is next on the list, and it's an homage to *Star Trek*. Martin takes a phone call and tells SG-1 that one of the new junior executives at the network has suggested they re-cast the whole movie with younger, edgier versions of the team. Cut to a young Teal'c, Mitchell, Carter, Daniel and Vala speaking in slang, where Vala is pregnant. Unsurprisingly, this isn't a big hit either. Vala puts more ideas forward, but each and every one is a rip-off. She tries *Gilligan's Island*, and then *Farscape* – with Carter as Chiana, Teal'c as D'Argo, Jackson as Crichton, herself as Aeryn, Thor as Rygel, and Mitchell as Stark. But the team are getting impatient, waiting for the gate to activate. When Martin tells them he is out of actors, Mitchell says that it's a fact of parallel dimension physics that each person exists somewhere in some universe in whatever shape or form you can imagine. Thus the team suggests that Martin could do

Above: *"Why can't we just go fishing?"*

the film without actors, but with puppets instead. Martin's not buying it. He's worried about the budget, as the actors are asking for money that he can't afford to give them. He says that he needs to rewrite the script with a twist in order to stroke their egos. And in a parallel twist, O'Neill walks into the meeting room. Teal'c's vision is a show about himself in a trench coat with a hat and earrings. He's a man "keepin' the streets safe, while keepin' it real." It's *Teal'c P.I.* Again, Martin is nonplussed. When asked about his unexpected visit, O'Neill says he feels as though he still has unfinished business... he needs closure at the SGC. Mitchell invites him to join them on his two hundredth step through the gate, and O'Neill seems enthused. Martin's next problem is that the focus group hates the film's ending and he has to change that too. O'Neill suggests they go fishing at the end, but it isn't a popular pitch. So Vala suggests a wedding between O'Neill and Carter. Daniel is the Best Man and Vala is the Maid of Honor. Landry interrupts to say that the gate is up and running – much to Martin's disappointment, as he has no ending for his film. O'Neill invites Landry to join them on the mission, who in turn invites Harriman to come along. Stargate teams 3 to 18 are waiting with balloons and streamers on the other side of the gate in celebration of Mitchell's two hundredth trip. Just as they are about to leave, O'Neill asks Martin to come along and see if he can find some inspiration for the end of his movie. But Martin has just had a call from the studio – the movie's been cancelled... they decided to renew the series instead. Å

(See page 100 for an in-depth look at the making of this episode.)

Counterstrike

Written by: Joseph Mallozzi & Paul Mullie

Directed by: Andy Mikita

Guest Cast: Tony Amendola (Bra'tac), Richard Whiten (Bo'rel), David Andrews (Se'tak)

SG-1 go undercover on a planet converting to Origin where a grown-up Adria addresses the villagers. As she stresses the importance of the words of the Orici, the *Odyssey* picks up an energy reading from the surface of the planet – a wave of radiation is emanating from the gate. SG-1 are beamed out just before all life on the planet is destroyed. The weapon used only targeted living tissue, and there is only one device that works in this way – the superweapon built by the Ancients. Bra'tac arrives at SGC and tells Landry that it was the Jaffa that deployed the weapon. Their new leader, Se'tak, convinced the council on Dakara that their only hope for survival against the armies of the Ori was to attack them using the Ancient device – murdering thousands of innocent villagers as well as Adria. Meanwhile SG-1 beam onto an unmanned and unguarded Ori ship. Mitchell and Teal'c find a power generation chamber where they plant C4, and Carter discovers that the main command interface is a chair which is probably keyed to the Priors' unique brain physiology. Teal'c and Mitchell encounter Bo'rel of the Free Jaffa who lays claim to the ship. Bo'rel seizes Mitchell's radio and broadcasts for a surrender, or he will harm Teal'c and Mitchell. Daniel answers, and suggests that they work together, but he and Vala are captured by a Jaffa patrol. Having survived the radiation thanks to a pendant which holds part of the city of Celestis, Adria arrives and tortures a Jaffa to find out where the Ancient weapon is. The Ori ship takes flight but Carter manages to beam SG-1 onto the *Odyssey*, before Adria turns the ship's weapons on Dakara. Back at the SGC, SG-1 receive word that not only has Dakara been destroyed, but five more planets have fallen to the Ori. The Merlin device is the only shot they have at stopping them.

Vala: Okay. We all know, darling, that you have telekinetic powers. You can stop showing off now.

'Counterstrike' marks actress Morena Baccarin's first appearance as adult Orici super-villain Adria. First choice to play season ten's new bad guy, Baccarin is best known for her role as Inara Serra in the science fiction television series *Firefly* and the follow-up film *Serenity*. For the writers and producers at *Stargate SG-1*'s Bridge Studio, the addition of Baccarin was

something to be excited about.

"'Counterstrike' is the first time we see Morena," shares the episode's co-writer Paul Mullie. "She was one of our first ideas to play Adria – we really didn't go through a lot of names for that part. I think we just got lucky in that we had an idea, and it worked out. We're all huge fans of *Firefly* – the DVDs have made their way round our office. Jewel Staite, of course, is on *Stargate: Atlantis* now, and we've tried to get other people from the show over here. We were very excited to get Morena onboard – she's been great."

With Adria's full-grown status comes her full-blown attempt to spread the word of the Ori throughout the galaxy.

"The idea was to give the Ori a face," explains Mullie. "Aside from the Priors, they were faceless because they didn't have a physical embodiment.

Above: This time, Vala is really stuck in the middle.

We always knew that was a problem as a villain. So we had this villain that you couldn't see or touch, and we needed to find a way around that. They do have representatives that think and act on their behalf, but it's not really them. Adria wasn't technically them either, but she was at least a face to them, and I think it helped crystallize that whole problem."

In addition to giving the Ori a face, the decision to give Adria a pre-established relationship with one of *Stargate SG-1*'s main characters certainly helped authenticate season ten's major story arc.

"There's already a personal bond there between Adria and Vala, which we hadn't originally planned," says Mullie. "Claudia got pregnant, so it was like, 'Okay... how are we going to work this in? Alright – she's having the child of the Ori.' There were some people who were worried about certain parallels to certain religions, but we decided not to worry too much about that. It was just kind of an obvious way to deal with her pregnancy really, and then when it came time to cast the part of Adria, we had to buy that she was Vala's daughter to a certain extent. I think Morena fits the bill."

Vala: Well, as your mother, I'm putting my foot down. You're too young to have your own army.

"This was a continuation of our attempt to rehabilitate Vala which we had started in 'Morpheus'," adds co-writer Joe Mallozzi. "Her relationships with Adria and with Daniel are explored again in 'Counterstrike'. We had put the Jaffa story to bed in season nine when they finally had their freedom, but it was nice to be able to use the Jaffa story again. There's no such thing as a happy ending. Granted they had their freedom, but there were other problems – now they had to deal with the Ori army. As is often the case in real life, with the former Soviet Union for example, you have your freedom, but there is still a more conservative element driving the issue. In this case, the Jaffa wipe out a human world because they think there are no other means of preventing the Ori army from continuing their encroachment on the galaxy. It was a huge episode!"

Director Will Waring admits that 'Counterstrike' was a much larger episode than it was initially intended to be. Having already seen the Ori ship in the season ten premiere, 'Flesh and Blood', Waring was excited to shoot in the new set.

"'Counterstrike' ended up being a little bit more than what we were expecting, even whilst we were shooting it," shares the director. "One of the great things about the episode was the set – the Ori ship that James Robbins had built in our Norco facility. You can shoot it any number of ways and it's

not a big deal in terms of lighting. You can shoot 360 degrees from big wide
angles to super-close and you don't have to change anything. It's limited in
terms of how much set there is, but the design meant you could turn
multiple corners, cut and then pick up the scene again. This gives the
illusion that it was a much bigger ship than the set would actually indicate.

"I didn't think the episode was going to have such a grand feel to it. It
had pretty extensive visual effects, and that always makes a huge difference.
When we can cut to big special effects like that, that can save our asses in a
big way if things are a little tighter and slower on set."

The biggest challenge, says Waring, was shooting within the same
physical space while trying to make the scenes look different.

"We had this one little section of the set that we were changing from one
holding room to another. We had to shoot everything relating to one of
those spaces first, and then move out, and the set decorators would come
in and change it all over. It worked, but it gives me the impression when I'm
shooting it that it's going to be boring. You can be doing ten, twelve or fifteen
scenes, but it feels like you're doing the same thing all over again, when in
fact you're not, and you have to keep that perspective. That was another
episode that when I saw it, I was like, 'This is actually pretty good!' I never
said it wasn't going to be strong, or be as good as the script, but once I saw
it put together, I felt really happy with it." Λ

Memento Mori

Written by: Joe Mallozzi & Paul Mullie Directed by: Peter DeLuise	Guest Cast: Patricia Harras (Fake Carter), Peter Benson (Devon), Sean Owen Roberts (Driver), Brian Davies (Waiter), Heather Christie (Waitress), Adrian Holmes (Detective Ryan), Don Stark (Sal), Sonya Salomaa (Athena), Brendan Beiser (Weaver), Phillip Mitchell (Guy #1)

D aniel rewards Vala's hard work by taking her to a fancy restaurant for dinner. But Vala is kidnapped and taken to Charlotte Mayfield, aka Athena – an old rival of Qetesh's, the Goa'uld that once occupied Vala's body. Athena wants the code to an Ancient tablet that Quetesh knew, and she has a device to help her locate the suppressed memories in Vala's mind. Meanwhile, Landry has the local authorities searching the area, and sends five teams to check out different suspected safehouses. SG-15 run into armed resistance where Vala is held, and during the attack the memory machine attached to Vala is hit with a zat blast. Confused and frightened, Vala makes her escape as the warehouse explodes. The only other survivor is a Trust operative, who tells SG-1 that Vala was being held at that location but that she managed to escape. Wandering the streets lost and hungry, Vala enters a diner and tries to leave without paying the bill. Confessing that she has amnesia, she is taken in by the diner's owner, Sal, who gives her a job as a waitress. One of Sal's customers, a policeman named Ryan, witnesses Vala incapacitating two robbers and takes her to the local police station for questioning. He files a missing person report, which both Landry and Athena see. Before SG-1 arrive, the Trust, disguised as Air Force personnel, accost Vala. Mitchell gives chase, while Vala escapes the Trust by forcing them to crash the car. Having taken Mitchell hostage, the amnesiac Vala demands answers, but thinks he's crazy when he tries to explain that she is an alien who works for the Stargate program. Having shot Mitchell in the shoulder and fled again, Vala hides out in an abandoned warehouse, but is soon located by both SG-1 and the Trust. A firefight ensues and Vala tries to run but is stopped by Daniel, who jogs her memory. Returning to the SGC, Vala is given an SG-1 patch. She's an official member of the team.

Vala: Oh, I've watched enough of your television to know what a date is. It's a romantic event, typified by dinner, movie and/or karaoke, and usually culminating in a night of...
Daniel: Uhh, okay, this is definitely not a date.

'Memento Mori' was penned by the writing/producing duo of Joseph Mallozzi and Paul Mullie, and endeavored to show how far Vala had come in terms of her importance to the SG-1 team. She may have started as a mild annoyance, but by the time 'Memento Mori' came around, it was clear that it was time for the character to be officially accepted as a part of the SGC.

Above: Worried: SG-1 contemplate life without Vala.

"That's basically charting Vala's progress further," agrees Mallozzi. "In 'Morpheus', it's her trying to prove herself to be part of the team, 'Counterstrike' is her out with the team, and here she eventually comes to be accepted as part of the team and gets her SG-1 badge."

Interestingly enough, the episode gave the audience a chance to see Vala in a guise her non-amnesiac self would have been most accustomed to: being on the run.

"She's a character who has always been on the run, so it's like second nature to her," Mallozzi explains. "So we decided to put her in a scenario where she's on the run on Earth, and while she's on the run we see how concerned the team is. Specifically Daniel, who has developed this relationship with Vala and has connected with her on a personal level. You see it's not just concern for a co-worker, but at least a close friend. We get to see his obsession with trying to track her down. That was another fun episode. We like to write for Vala. In general, any opportunity you have to show the camaraderie between team-members is always great. Claudia and Michael have a definite chemistry between them and knowing that they will be able to hit it out of the park makes writing those type of scenes very easy."

Though their frequency has increased over more recent seasons, Earth-based episodes are still fairly rare for *Stargate SG-1*. As the writers explain, writing science fiction stories on imaginary worlds is far easier – after all, the audience can't contradict what the writers choose to create. But on Earth, in the present day, fitting in believable science fiction elements makes the suspension of disbelief that much more fragile.

"I loved that episode, actually," says Paul Mullie. "Again, I like character-driven episodes, episodes that deal with how people relate to each other but still have action and still have a sci-fi element. To be honest, it's really not that easy, and it's not even that it's Earth based – that's another problem. To do a character-driven episode that still has all those other elements and still works as an action-adventure is really hard, so when they do work out, it's always gratifying. I like it when we can get away with Earth-based episodes because I know that they are difficult. It was always a challenge to make them exciting and have an interesting jeopardy. The fact that we can get all that, and also have a character-driven story made it particularly gratifying for me."

Daniel: You don't remember who you are, but I do... You've been running so long it's almost second nature to you. You don't remember it, but you made a decision to stop running. It's over. Now it's time to come home.

"Whenever we're doing the Earth-based stuff, it's always very tricky," adds Mallozzi. "If you go off-world, you're dealing with the sci-fi concept. You go and you come back. But when you're on Earth you're dealing with the Trust, or very specific Earth-based bad guys, and you want to include a sci-fi element in the show. Often that's easier said than done, but in this case, Vala's the alien and she possesses this knowledge, and we throw in Athena. It was the best of both worlds, having the sci-fi backstory and [having] SG-1 on an Earth-based adventure."

Setting an SG-1 episode firmly on Earth also changes the nature of the pre-production process for the art department.

"Episodes like that automatically become location shows," James Robbins explains, "because the standing stages that we have, most of them are dedicated to stuff that is already established in the SGC and in Atlantis and the ships. So rather than build those we go to locations and dress the locations. For 'Memento Mori', we went to a diner and we didn't have to do a whole lot there – you just change your tables around and put up some graphics: we put that sign outside on the street to emulate some other sort of place. We went to the restaurant and the high-end office where the female executive Goa'uld worked; those are both actually boardrooms in a hotel downtown. We turned one into a restaurant with a big graphic outside the door, a concierge stand, a few twinkle lights and trees inside and it was all good!"

For the office set, however, a little more set designing magic was required. "We actually did a bit of a build in the office area," Robbins reveals. "Some things are just quite iconic and distinctive, and you walk into most boardrooms and it just feels like a boardroom, so we had to make some changes in there to make it a little more high-end. You get the sense of a high-end office if you are actually very high up. She had a nice view of other buildings and business towers downtown out of her window and that kind of helped sell the look."

Above: *"Valerie" tries to remember her past.*

Robbins reports that it was the set-decorating department that had the most intensive job during the shoot. Having found the locations, it was their task to fill them with appropriate props, which, along with the rest of the sets, had to be 'struck', or removed completely the next day.

"Quite honestly, I think I prefer to build," confesses the designer. "It's always best to work in sets as opposed to actual locations, because you don't have a lighting grid over the top, so it's tough to light people. You have to try to hide things. And none of the walls move. In our sets, I try to design everything so that the walls can come away whenever we need them to so that you can get back with the camera or hide a light or do whatever you need to do. So shooting in locations isn't as film-friendly. But it is easy to get a lot of different looks, and that's why we go there – for me to build all those different environments would have been cost prohibitive, that's really what it comes down to." Å

Company of Thieves

Written by: Alan McCullough Directed by: William Waring	Guest Cast: Rudolf Martin (Anateo), Eric Steinberg (Netan), Adrien Dorval (Borzin), Hawthorne James (Gavos), Michael Rogers (Major Escher), Dean Monroe Mckenzie (Teresh), Joey Aresco (Slaviash), Scott McNeil (Kefflin), Morris Chapdelaine (Tenat), Sean Campbell (Solek), Timothy Paul Perez (Vashin), Geoff Redknap (Oranian Lieutenant)

With Carter, Marks and Colonel Emerson onboard, the *Odyssey* is ambushed by three Goa'uld motherships and driven into a minefield, where the ship is seriously damaged. Colonel Emerson radios Stargate Command to inform Landry of the attack, but the *Daedalus* is on its way to Atlantis, leaving SG-1 without a ship. Solek boards the *Odyssey* and Carter and Emerson are taken to Anateo, who wears a Lucian Alliance uniform but claims to be no part of any alliance. He has found a subspace beacon giving away the ship's position, and he wants Carter to shut it off. Emerson orders her not to help them, and is subsequently killed. Meanwhile the rest of SG-1 are onboard a poor quality ship and their long-range sensors indicate that the signal coming from the *Odyssey* transponder is changing location and traveling at sub-light speed. Their sensors pick up life signs on another planet and Vala recognizes it as being inhabited by the Goa'uld's former human slaves, who have ties with the Lucian Alliance. Vala has a contact there called Borzin, and she and Daniel ask Borzin if he has any information about a Tau'ri ship that was attacked. As he shows them the *Odyssey's* data recorder, Vala and Daniel are captured by Solek and taken to Anateo onboard the *Odyssey*. Mitchell decides to infiltrate the Lucian Alliance by posing as Kefflin, one of Netan's most loyal and reclusive lieutenants. By using the Reole chemical on Netan, Netan believes Mitchell to be whoever he says he is. Vala and Daniel escape the *Odyssey's* cargo bay but Anateo threatens to shoot Carter unless they surrender immediately. Vala responds by beaming him into space. Onboard the Lucian Alliance ship, Netan has captured Teal'c and is about to kill him when Tenat reports that they've found the *Odyssey*. Mitchell and Teal'c escape to Tenat's mothership and order him to open fire on the other Goa'uld ship. Mitchell and Teal'c beam aboard the *Odyssey* and declare war on the Lucian Alliance.

Teal'c: Perhaps they were trying to deter us from trying to find the *Odyssey*.
Mitchell: Personally, I think they just don't like us.

Fed up with the *Odyssey* coming to the rescue of SG-1, 'Company of Thieves' writer Alan McCullough decided it was time that SG-1 went to the rescue of the *Odyssey*.

"In many of my episodes, or many episodes just in general, we were saved at the last minute by the *Odyssey* or *Prometheus*," shares McCullough. "We were beamed out at the last second, and I thought it would be interesting if it was the other way round and we had no ship to help us. So I pitched that idea to the room, and eventually it got spun into 'Company of Thieves'."

Above: *'Company of Thieves' marks the end of Colonel Emerson (Matthew Glave).*

With so many last-minute escapes come just as many near-death experiences, and this episode also marks a significant demise for a certain recurring character. Colonel Paul Emerson, Commander of the *Odyssey* since season nine's 'Off the Grid', meets his match at the hands of Anateo.

"At the time in my outline, I had someone we didn't care about get shot," McCullough reveals. "But Rob was like, 'Well, we're going to have to kill someone we care about.' It obviously couldn't be Carter, so we lost Colonel Emerson in that episode. I wrote that into the script and that was the first time I killed someone off in the script that was a recurring character. I was pretty nervous about it – but at least it was our last season!"

With intermingled storylines, numerous ambushes and false identities, 'Company of Thieves' packs a lot of action into its fast-paced fifty minutes. How was the writing process of such a quick and detailed episode?

"Ultimately, 'Company of Thieves' was a fun episode to do," answers McCullough, "but for whatever reason, some episodes are really easy to write, and some are really difficult to write. 'Insiders' was really easy to write, but 'Company of Thieves' was very difficult. When I wrote the first draft, I took it into the writers' room and everyone had just read it. I could tell by the energy in the room that people didn't care for it much, and so I got hundreds and hundreds of notes and I went right back to the drawing board. I wrote a second draft which went over a lot better, but it slowed me down considerably." He laughs. "I took a great deal of time over the second draft because you don't want to have that reaction twice!"

Mitchell: You should probably add that we have officially declared war on the Lucian Alliance.

With so much of season ten's story arc heavily focused on the Ori, 'Company of Thieves' acts as an important reminder to the viewers of the presence of lawless renegades the Lucian Alliance. Maybe not as big, bad or certainly as ugly as the Ori's Priors, the Sopranos of science fiction are nonetheless a force to be reckoned with.

"I wanted to get into the Lucian Alliance more because I wanted to explore them the way you would explore the Mob. They're really the galaxy's Mafia," points out McCullough. "We'd sort of touched on that and they were an evil kind of conglomerate, but it was quite shady, and I really wanted to do an episode where we get into the guts of what their structure is. Who leads? How do they divide their territory? So this episode allowed us to go undercover and go inside the Lucian Alliance and get to know them a little bit. That's what makes the show great. You have an unlimited canvas

Above: Carter is held at gunpoint... again.

on which to paint on, and you develop this mythology which is the best place to find story ideas. You look at something which is just sort of casually mentioned in one episode and you say, 'Well, what is that? Let's take a closer look and see if we can build an episode from that section of the mythology.' So yeah, obviously the Ba'al clones led to a story, the Lucian Alliance led to a story, all the stories are like that.

"I thought it was a really good episode," the writer continues. "Some of the best lines I can't take credit for, because when Rob did a pass he added in a bunch of things, like, 'Damn you, Cam Mitchell!' All those moments with the alien Jup were his. Some of the best lines came from Robert Cooper. I was very pleased with how that episode eventually turned out."

For director Will Waring, 'Company of Thieves' also proved quite problematic at first. Basing the episode onboard various ships was certainly the most challenging aspect the director faced.

"There's only so much spaceship that exists that we have on set, so you're constantly switching stuff around to make it fit," shares Waring. "The ship we used to have had three times as much spaceship available to us in terms of room, so in your mind you always have that as the backdrop and you mentally place where you can put things. Then you go to the stage and you realise, 'Oh, that's right, we don't have that, we've only got one corridor, one big room and the bridge,' and that's essentially all you've got. It's hard to make those sets appear as more than what they are, but it always works and you always buy into it. It's just that at the time, you worry about how to get around it. I was very pleased at how it actually turned out in the end." Å

The Quest [Part I]

Written by: Joe Mallozzi & Paul Mullie Directed by: Andy Mikita	Guest Cast: Doug Abrahams (Prior), Beverley Breuer (Barkeep), Quinn Lord (Young Boy), Kenton Reid (Ori Soldier), Rod Loomis (Osric), Steve Archer (Ori Commander), Stephen Holmes (Villager)

The quest for the Holy Grail continues as Daniel discovers that the coordinates of the planets visited by King Arthur and his knights form a perfect pyramid. Claiming the answer came to her in a dream, Vala reveals that the planet on which the Sangraal is located can be determined by combining the addresses of Castiana, Sahal and Vagonbrei. SG-1 gate to the planet and enter a medieval village, similar to Camelot. They find that they're the second group of adventurers in less than a week to take up the quest for the Sangraal. A number of Jaffa, led by Ba'al, passed through three days ago. The team are warned that no one has ever returned from the quest alive, and that they must consult with the parchment of virtues in the village library to prepare them for the journey ahead. In the library they meet Osric, keeper of the village archives. He shows them a parchment which was left behind by Morgan Le Fay as a guide for knights of noble spirit who demonstrate prudence, charity, kindness, wisdom, and faith. The Sangraal will belong to whoever speaks the guardian's name. The guardian is said to be a powerful dragon, but SG-1 are skeptical. Osric claims to know the way to the Sangraal and leads SG-1 to the cave where it resides. They meet Ba'al along the way, and allow him to accompany them as he claims to know the dragon's name. Jackson discovers that Osric is not who he appears to be, as he paraphrases the book of Origin. He is, in fact, Adria in disguise. She needs Daniel to help her acquire the Ancient weapon, and threatens to kill the team. They are subjected to a series of tests until they reach the Sangraal. As Daniel attempts to pick it up, his hand goes straight through it, and the cave begins to shake. The passageway closes behind them, and above them swoops a huge dragon, breathing fire, and ready to attack...

Vala: We agreed there's no such thing as a dragon, right?
Mitchell: Yeah.
Vala: Hmm... Because that looks pretty real to me.

The mid-season two-parter is particularly impressive in scope. More like a game of *Dungeons & Dragons* than a TV show, the script had everyone talking – from the visual effects department to the cast and producers.

Bursting with high fantasy elements, 'The Quest, Part I' was written by writing duo Joe Mallozzi and Paul Mullie. A self-confessed fantasy and science fiction fan, the episode was a dream come true for the ever imaginative Mallozzi, who is renowned for his knowledge of all things fantastical.

Above: *The Priors show they mean business.*

"We had two very different episodes," Mallozzi explains. "'The Quest, Part I' is very camp. Anyone who has played fantasy role-playing computer games, or read fantasy books, will recognize a lot of it. One of the things that really made it fun was including Ba'al. Cliff Simon does such a terrific job as Ba'al – he's my alter ego. He's a lot of fun to write for. I also really enjoyed writing the riddles, and there was a great magical element to the episode, culminating in a dragon at the end! I prefer the less hands-on, more practical riddles. Rob [Cooper] really likes the puzzles, which I'm not very good at, but I guess we all have our forte."

The riddles take up a large part of the episode, and while SG-1 manage to work their way through them in a decent time, surely it took Mallozzi longer to come up with them?

"The riddles didn't take as much time as you would think," he smiles. "You have to be in the mood for it, and I have the experience of playing *Dungeons & Dragons* when I was younger. I did a little research on some of the virtues – prudence, charity, kindness, wisdom, and faith. Originally I wanted to do one virtue for each character, but it didn't work out."

"You had more riddles at first," Mullie chips in. "We had to cut some because there just wasn't enough time. I can't stand writing that stuff. When Joe was pitching that story, I was like, 'Okay, have fun!' All those puzzles and riddles – they're fun to watch, but I find them very tiresome to write, so Joe basically had to come up with most of that himself. I really liked the box riddle with Ba'al, though – that was a good one. I'm terrible with coming up with things like that, and Robert Cooper's always writing these riddle episodes too."

Osric: Truth is elusive to those who refuse to see with both eyes wide.

A team episode, 'The Quest, Part I' was a huge hit with the viewers – most likely because it had all the cast together for almost every scene. But it wasn't just the five core members of SG-1… Adding Ba'al and Adria to the mix makes great viewing, but it also makes the director's job far more difficult.

"Whenever you get them all together, it's a pain in the ass," laughs Mikita. "Just trying to get all the cast members at the same place at the same time is a challenge unto itself. To have that many people that you have to do coverage for takes a long time. The writers were teasing me; they were like, 'If you think you hate us now, wait till you read 'The Quest'!' Every cast member is in every scene, plus Cliff Simon and Morena are in it. There were seven people in every scene, so that was the big challenge of that episode."

Dubbed 'Monty Python's Quest for the Holy Grail', the episode was not just a big hit with the fans – it was also memorable for the cast who, after ten years together, still relish every opportunity they get to work as a team.

Above: *Face-off. Ba'al and Adria size each other up.*

"'The Quest, Part I' was really fun," Michael Shanks remembers. "You had this bunch of morons wandering around the forest, completely mismatched, searching for the Sangraal, complete with dragon and whatnot! It's kind of out of the realm of what we're used to on this show, so that was just a lot of fun to do. I know that the director, poor Andy Mikita, was bashing his head against the wall, day-in, day-out, because he had so many people in the same room all the time and all the coverage that came with it. But all of us getting to hang together for the episode was a lot of fun."

Big visual effects and numerous castmembers weren't the only challenges facing Mikita. Just when everything seems to be under control, you can always count on Mother Nature to stir things up…

"We had a tough time shooting the time dilation field scene!" laughs Mikita. "The big issue was that we had hired actors to stand perfectly still as they were supposed to be trapped in the dilation field, moving so slowly that they looked to be frozen. But the leaves were blowing in the wind! So we put in some dialogue to cover it up. There was also a hole in one of the trees with a bird and her chicks. You could hear it chirping and the bird would fly out, get food and fly back into the tree – through the time dilation field! So it was quite funny. I'm not sure if you can see it on camera on the final cut – you have to go back and have a look! There was so much to do in this episode and with no extra time. But it was a great script, lots of fun, and I loved the whole premise of it." Å

The Quest [Part II]

Written by: Joseph Mallozzi & Paul Mulllie **Directed by:** Andy Mikita	**Guest Cast:** Doug Abrahams (Prior), Steve Archer (Ori Commander), Matthew Walker (Merlin)

Trapped in a cave with a fire-breathing dragon, Adria protects Ba'al and SG-1 by covering them in a force-field. The dragon swings its tail and creates an opening in the wall, through which the team escapes – but the dragon bursts through the top of the cave. Ba'al had lied about knowing the guardian's secret name, but as the dragon attacks, Daniel works out the name is Morgan Le Fay – Ganos Lal in Ancient. He speaks it aloud and the dragon disappears. They return to the chamber which contains the Sangraal, but once again, Jackson's hand passes straight through it. There is a flash of light and all but Adria are transported into another chamber. Merlin stands before them in an Ancient stasis chamber, and is released by Vala. As they wait for him to revive, Carter, Mitchell, Teal'c and Ba'al look for a way out of the room... but they weren't just transported to another chamber, but another planet. Merlin wakes up and thinks that SG-1 are knights of the round table, not realising that one thousand years have passed. He approaches the Ancient device in the wall, and puts his head into it. The small round table lights up and holograms of molecules appear. Teal'c calls the team outside – the gate has activated on its own and they seem to be on a completely different planet due to a deliberate alteration of the DHD program. Carter and Ba'al work together on the device, trying to figure out a way to dial out from the gate. Growing weaker with the stress of building the Sangraal, Merlin faces the Repository of the Ancients once more before he dies – downloading his knowledge into Daniel's mind so that he can finish building the weapon. Adria manages to track SG-1 down, but Daniel has enhanced mental powers and he strikes the Ori soldiers down. As he blocks an attack from Adria, the others manage to escape – the gate closes behind them, and Daniel is taken captive.

Ba'al: His little trick with my vocal chords expired when he died.
Teal'c: Yet another reason to mourn his passing.

Leaving SG-1 trapped in a cave with a dragon is a rather dramatic way to break for the hiatus. While 'The Quest, Part I' and 'The Quest, Part II' share the same prefix, they are rather dissimilar in both plot and pace. So if, as

according to writer Joe Mallozzi, 'The Quest, Part I' is "high fantasy camp"... *Above: Is it a bird? Is it a plane?*
what's the second part?

"Oh, the second part is very exciting," beams Mallozzi, whose enthusiasm for the mid-season two-parter is highly evident. And as far as "exciting" goes, you can't get much more exciting than having a dragon in your show.

Writing such a huge character into the script was certainly a brave move for the writers – and a big challenge for the effects team.

"Sometimes these creatures work out really well, sometimes they don't," shares Paul Mullie, who co-wrote the episode with Mallozzi. "We've had a mixed history on the show of doing purely CG creatures. We've done some Asgards which have been purely CG, and have been pretty good for the most part. We've done smaller creatures in CG – like the one in 'Morpheus' which I thought was pretty good. That little lizard was relatively small, but it looked good. The dragon worked really well in some shots, but not as well in others. There was a scale problem. When there was nothing to give him scale he didn't look as good. You go into these episodes knowing that you're taking a risk and it's probably not going to be perfect, but it was part of the story and it made sense to do it."

Before the episode was broadcast on television, Mallozzi had the fans on the edge of their seats, having written in his Gateworld blog: "The *SG-1* mid-season two-parter has the visual effects department salivating." But, as exciting as the prospect of a dragon was, it was a challenging prospect for director Andy Mikita.

"I thought the dragon was going to be bigger," shares Mikita. "The visual effects team did a great job on the dragon, but from some angles I thought it could have been bigger. One thing I thought was really great about this episode was that a lot of the scenes we shot looked like they had visual effects in them, but they were actually practical. When SG-1 go to all of these different planets where the Stargate is situated – on a desert planet, a forested planet and a snow covered planet – these were all practical on a stage, none of those were visual effects. It took some work, and it took some time to get it all changed over, as we were constantly moving in and out of the studio to allow the guys to change it all over. Those shows with that grand scale are so much fun. I think I ended up getting an extra day between those two episodes as it was such a huge episode. In that same physical environment where we had the Stargate was the Sangraal. That was the same set which had to be changed again. A lot of that was visual effects as well, where they took away the floor, and made it into a big *Lord of the Rings*-style cavern."

Mitchell: You don't get fancy mind powers unless there has been major redecorating going on inside your skull!

Indeed the effects make for quite a dramatic episode, but as usual, it was the character moments within the drama that made 'The Quest, Part II' such a joy to watch. As Daniel begins to lose more of himself to Merlin, Vala finds herself facing a situation where she has to watch someone she cares about suffer. During her attempts to help him, her fellow teammates seem far more composed than she is. It is with this realisation of how much Vala cares for her new friends, that Mitchell announces she is now officially a member of SG-1 in his mind: the hardest part about being a member of the team is not risking your own life, it's watching your friends take chances with theirs.

Above: Vala fears for Daniel's health.

Her despair is perhaps the most engrossing part of the episode.

"'The Quest, Part II' is a lot more character-driven than 'The Quest, Part I'," says Mallozzi. "There are some really nice scenes between Vala and Mitchell which shows her concern for Daniel. It all mirrors Daniel's concern for her when she went missing in 'Memento Mori' – now it's her concern for Daniel losing his mind in this episode."

By facing the Repository of the Ancients, Daniel downloads Merlin's knowledge into his brain and begins to undergo a transformation. This part of the story sets up Daniel's – or should we say Michael Shanks' – disappearance in the later episodes of the season.

"That was the other challenge," explains Mallozzi. "As Michael Shanks was only contracted to do sixteen episodes, we had to begin writing him out. Part of the agenda of that story was having him getting taken at the end of the episode."

This was a controversial story arc for Daniel, which culminated in him becoming a Prior in 'The Shroud'.

"It's a way to justify the two episodes in the summer that I'm taking off," laughs Shanks, "but at the same time it's a great story development idea where Daniel goes over to the other side for a little bit, and everybody has to deal with the ramifications of that." Å

Line in the Sand

Written by: Alan McCullough Directed by: Peter DeLuise	Guest Cast: Aisha Hinds (Thilana), Aaron Craven (Matar), Greg Anderson (Prior), Sean Tyson (Ori Firstman), Tim Guinee (Tomin)

In a briefing with Colonel Reynolds, SG-1 are informed that the inhabitants of P9C-882 were visited by a Prior, who has told them to build a device which is used to burn people alive. The villagers reject the ways of the Ori; having lived under the Goa'uld for centuries, they are determined to remain free. They need Merlin's cloaking device to make them disappear before the Prior returns in three days. SG-1 and Colonel Reynolds gate to P9C-882 where they are greeted by the village leader, Thilana. Carter activates the cloaking device, and the village disappears, but later the displacement field collapses due to a power disruption. Carter rigs an Ancient capacitor between the device and the generators to collect the power and hopefully feed it more evenly, but she runs out of time as Ori fighter ships fly overhead. She attempts to fix the device, but is shot by an Ori soldier. Carter truly believes that she's not going to make it, but she and Mitchell manage to activate the device and the building vanishes. Outside, Tomin appears, ordering that Vala be taken to the Ori ship, and many of the villagers are killed. Those who remain seek shelter in another room in the village, but the soldiers enter and demand to know how the building in the village square disappeared. A Prior tells Tomin that they must destroy the village and kill the remaining unbelievers. But Tomin begins to question the interpretation of the Book of Origin, refusing to stand by whilst innocent people are massacred. Meanwhile, though Carter is growing weaker, she realizes that the crystal from an Ori staff can provide power for a short time. Tomin helps Vala escape, but when she walks back to where the village once stood, she finds a large hole in the ground caused by the blast. Suddenly, there's a blast of light and she finds herself in the village center surrounded by the villagers. Carter was able to expand the range of the device in time. She is taken back to the SGC infirmary and recuperates, much to the relief of a worried Mitchell.

Vala: Tomin, wait. There's one thing I want you to know that is the truth. There were real moments between us. I did fall in love with you.

"It was supposed to be a Carter-focused episode," explains writer Alan

Above: A Prior *examines Teal'c.*

McCullough of how 'Line in the Sand' developed before reaching the screen. "But then the way the story unfolded – the Vala storyline got brought up and it became a team episode with people caught in different places. Everybody was in some kind of jeopardy. I really enjoyed and liked the way that episode turned out."

Though the episode expanded to bring in all the show's main characters, McCullough still found plenty of time to explore a new aspect of Colonel Carter's psyche. Audiences have been watching Carter on screen for a decade and may feel that they know the character inside-out – yet 'Line in the Sand' still managed to reveal something new about the military career-woman and scientist.

"Carter's had her life threatened before, but not really to the point where she actually thinks she's going to die," McCullough explains. "We talked about it in the room, and it was like, 'What would Carter's relationship with God be? How would she be feeling? What do you feel when you're a scientist devoted to science your whole life; how does it feel at the end of your life when science has no more options for you?' That was a very interesting part of that episode for me."

Actress Amanda Tapping enjoyed the opportunity to show another side of Sam, and doesn't think that Carter's life choices, specifically her choice of career, preclude her having a spiritual side.

"The idea of faith and science can work together," says Tapping. "Carter is not an unreligious person. I think religion and science are not mutually exclusive and they do often go hand-in-hand."

Putting the character in mortal danger, the actress feels, also gave her pause for thought. "Carter has to make sure that she's giving due credence to the people in her life, because all of a sudden it dawns on her that this may really be it," she says. "I'm sure that as a military person you're prepared for that: 'There's my secret stash of letters; make sure they get delivered.'

Carter: I spent my entire life dedicated to science. Plus the last ten years trying to convince people they believed in false gods. I don't think science is gonna help me.

"'Line in the Sand' was a big one for me," Tapping continues. "The hardest part of that is playing her when she first gets shot and not wanting to go over the top with it, but give it due credence that she's actually in mortal danger. But you feel a bit dumb! You feel idiotic writhing around on the floor, moaning. You want to make it real but at the same time you feel a bit dumb. I thought that turned out pretty well though."

Another episode highlight for the actress was the interaction between Carter and Mitchell, which up until this point had not been as plentiful as the actress would have liked.

"I had great fun playing scenes with Ben," smiles Tapping. "Ben and I hadn't really had an opportunity to play a lot together and finally we got that opportunity in 'Line in the Sand'."

The episode also provided a somewhat daunting challenge for James Robbins and the art department. After all, the area in which Carter is lying injured is supposed to be 'out of phase' – and how do you illustrate invisibility on screen?

"That was quite a change out," Robbins reveals. "The whole thing with Merlin's keyboard – we discovered earlier – putting things out of phase. In the story it backfires and only part of one building, where Carter is in there injured with Mitchell, goes out of phase. So we talked about how we were going to achieve this, whether it was a visual effect. Ultimately, we wound up doing what made the most sense – we actually made the building go away! We built one room and then took all the walls away and built little sections which showed cut-outs through the walls, indicating the edge of the forcefield they were being held in. So we built it all, shot all the interiors, and then they went away and shot some other stuff on other stages. Then they came back and we'd struck the building and left the aftermath behind for all the scenes in which they were out of phase. That was kind of fun. Why cheat when you can have the real thing?"

Above: *Please sir... can we have some more?*

All in all, the finished episode of 'Line in the Sand' was popular with cast and crew alike.

"In my opinion that's my favorite script that I did," says McCullough. "That came off the cleanest. Peter DeLuise did a great job directing that episode, it felt like it had some weight to it. We had some great guest stars, which really helped. Some of those scenes were beefy scenes, and it's great that we can hire a guest star who rises to the challenge. Our lead cast did a great job too, of course."

"The only thing about 'Line in the Sand' that bugged me is that I don't think she should have been on a bed," reveals Tapping. "I know that they had cots and it made sense because they were staying in the village and obviously they'd have their own quarters, but it seemed almost too comfortable. I think it would have been more compelling if they had left her on the floor, but there she is with a pillow. That was my only thing – it's too comfortable. I should be on the floor. But I had a lot of fun, and Ben and I finally got that scene together which I really enjoyed." Å

The Road Not Taken

Story by: Alan McCullough	**Guest Cast:** Michael Chase (Chief of Staff), Billy
Directed by: Andy Mikita	Mitchell (Senator), Linda Bayliss (Senator's Wife), Travis
	Woloshyn (Protestor), Robert Mann (Dr Bennett),
	Alexander Boynton (Floor Director), Don S. Davis
	(General George Hammond), Kavan Smith (Major
	Lorne), David Hewlett (Dr Rodney McKay), Kendall Cross
	(Julia Donovan)

Carter is working on Merlin's phasing device in the hope that it can create a large phase-shifted field. As she continues her tests, she activates the device and disappears. Awakening in the SGC, Carter finds that she is trapped in a parallel reality where Major Lorne is the leader of SG-1, General George Hammond leads Stargate Command, and Hank Landry is President of the United States. In this universe, Daniel has been captured by the Ori, Mitchell quit the military, Teal'c went back to the Jaffa, Vala is occupying a cell in Area 51 and Carter was once married to Rodney McKay. The Carter from this reality (Major Carter) was developing a process to extract energy from parallel universes. At the precise moment that Major Carter tapped into Colonel Carter's reality, Colonel Carter's lab was out of phase and inside a force field. General Hammond tells Carter that the Ori attempted an attack on Earth and Major Carter was running the experiment as their ZPM was nearly depleted. Three years ago Anubis launched an attack on Earth and they had to reveal the existence of the Stargate program to the world. Now, the Ori are assembling a full-scale fleet to prepare for an attack on Earth. Based on experiments in her own reality, Carter manipulates the phasing field and hides the entire planet, saving them from the Ori. Carter seeks McKay's help to get home, as he and his sister built the bridge between parallel universes, but McKay is blackmailed by the government to stop him from helping her. Agreeing to appear on a television show, Carter says that she intends to push for improved foreign relations and the restoration of civil liberties that were lost since the President took office. In the middle of her speech, the television show is cut off. McKay is given the role as special advisor to the President and his first order of business is to create an inter-universal bridge… and Carter is sent home.

Alternate Hammond: I understand you're coming to see certain things about this world that you don't like. To tell the truth, we don't much like them either.

'The Road Not Taken' asks an incredibly significant question… What would happen if the Stargate program became public? An undercover government/military initiative, the Stargate programme works under the radar of public knowledge. Were the media to find out about it, it would be certain to cause general uproar, mass hysteria and diplomatic fallout. As a question which has taken ten years to ask, is it something that writer Alan McCullough had been interested in exploring since he first joined *Stargate SG-1*'s prolific writing team?

"Well, the story actually came about in a different way," explains McCullough. "I had originally pitched a story where Carter gets sent into another reality and kills her other self in that reality, and then wants to leave but she isn't allowed. That was just the basis of the pitch, and

Above: President Landry looks to the future.

then Rob [Cooper] suggested that in this reality, the Stargate program is public, and we could explore what effect that would have. I came back to my office after we'd had a general talk about it, and I thought, 'Well, the first thing I want to do is have Mitchell in a wheelchair.' So I went and asked Rob if it was okay to have our lead in a wheelchair. That anti-hero who has given up, he's depressed, he's lost all the qualities that we love about him. Rob was like, 'Yeah, totally do it.' After I wrote my first draft, Rob read it and said, 'I thought you were going to make Mitchell like Lieutenant Dan [from *Forrest Gump*]. I want it *Born on the Fourth of July!*' I had pulled back in the writing of it because I was concerned about how far to take it. But they all read my first draft and they said, 'Go further! Go further! Make it more dirty, more despairing.'

Actor Ben Browder certainly rose to the challenge, and it's a very memorable scene for his character. Director Andy Mikita points out Browder's performance as a highlight of the episode.

"When Carter went to Mitchell's apartment, Mitchell's smoking, he has long hair, and he's in a wheelchair. I thought Ben did a great job of it," shares Mikita. "It was interesting because I'd never seen Ben do Method acting before, but it was really interesting to watch him. He was working it over in his head and after we'd rehearsed it, he was standing outside and actually smoking these cigarettes – he doesn't smoke! It was quite neat to see him really invest himself into the role. It was fun rehearsing the scene because it was well written and pretty dramatic."

Sam: The Rodney I know is a master of subtle persuasion. **Alternate McKay:** Hmm. Oh, you're lying again, aren't you?

For Browder, playing the fallen hero was a refreshing departure from his usual portrayal of the enthusiastic and eager Mitchell.

"I was smoking the cigarettes because I was afraid if I stopped I was going to throw up!" laughs Browder. "I figured as long as I kept smoking it would be okay. It's more difficult to stop and start again. I was literally smoking cigarettes for about three hours and for days afterwards I was scraping tar off my tongue – I don't recommend that as a method! But I wanted to visually show how far Mitchell had fallen, and it's not something I think we've ever seen from any *Stargate SG-1* character in any episode anywhere. I was like, 'Gump, you ruined my life! Gump, I was supposed to die in 'Nam!'"

By staying true to the mythology but messing up the timeline, McCullough created a whole new history for these people. Much of it never made the screen, but Ben Browder wasn't the only actor to relish his new role: Beau Bridges played the part of the President.

"I can't take credit for that," admits McCullough. "Originally it was supposed to be William Devane, who played President Hayes in our reality, but after we'd done all the drafts, we tried to book him for the episode, but he was not available. So there was sort of a panic, where everyone was like, 'What are we going to do? We can't bring in anyone new, because that won't carry any weight, there's no resonance to that whatsoever.' It was Rob who came up with the idea of making it Landry. It turned out better than we could have hoped for. Ultimately the line more or less stays the same, but it made that episode really interesting. It

Above: Rodney McKay (David Hewlett) helps his "estranged wife".

was someone we knew, who was a really good person in our reality. Beau really ate it up. He kept coming up to my office to talk about it before it was shot, and he wanted me to run lines with him a few times. He'd sit on the couch, and I'd read lines from Carter or Hammond, and he was loving it. He suggested little tweaks here and there, and really took it seriously – which I think shows in the episode as well."

Accepting that Carter, along with the other familiar characters, was actually in a parallel reality wasn't as easy as mixing up the roles. In order to believe the story, we too had to feel out of our comfort zone.

"The art department changed things very subtly in this episode," tells Mikita. "The set had to be the same, yet slightly different. We ended up relighting all the sets just enough to make you feel a little bit uneasy and everyone felt guarded. It was a little bit darker, and that was the tone we were going for overall. We changed little things to try and portray that it wasn't the same reality. Hats off to the lighting and the art department – they did a great job." Å

The Shroud

Story by: Robert C. Cooper	Guest Cast: Richard Dean Anderson (Major General
Directed by: Andy Mikita	Jack O'Neill), Robert Picardo (Richard Woolsey),
	Christopher Gaze (Trevaris)

SG-1 gate to a planet that has recently been visited by a Prior preaching the Book of Origin. On the Prior's return, the team take cover and watch him pull off his hood to reveal... Daniel Jackson. Daniel is beamed aboard the Odyssey and Mitchell zats him, rendering him unconscious. He is restrained and an anti-Prior device is used to stop him using his powers. Claiming he still has Merlin's consciousness in his mind, Daniel explains that letting himself become a Prior was part a plan to get Adria to trust him so that he could steal an Ori ship and fly it through the Supergate to the Ori galaxy with the completed weapon onboard and destroy them. But there's a wormhole blocking the Supergate and Daniel needs SG-1 to shut it down. General O'Neill is briefed at SGC of Daniel's transformation, and they discuss the possibility that Daniel's plan could be an elaborate plot to get them to shut down the wormhole, enabling more Ori ships into their galaxy. Based on Woolsey's recommendation, the IOA has proposed to the President that Daniel Jackson's life be immediately terminated. SG-1 (minus Daniel and O'Neill) beam aboard the Ori device to finish what Daniel cannot, but Daniel breaks out of his restraints and beams O'Neill onboard – he's taking the ship to make sure the mission is completed. On the Ori ship, Vala finishes the assembling of the weapon, but an Ori vessel is guarding the Supergate and Adria is now onboard. Jackson beams onto the bridge of the Ori vessel and knocks Adria out with a burst of energy and an anti-Prior device. The weapon and the gate are activated, and the Ori ship that was guarding it moves away, as the ship with the device aboard moves towards it. Jackson returns to his original form exhausted, and the team is beamed out, leaving Adria behind as the Ori ship moves through the gate. Onboard the *Odyssey*, Daniel recovers, and as the team wonder if the weapon was successful, the Supergate dials up before them. From the bridge the team watch as six Ori ships come through and enter hyperspace...

Opposite: Four against two – hardly a fair fight!

O'Neill: Alright, listen to me closely, 'cause I'm only gonna say this once. You kill Daniel... over my dead body!

A firm fan favorite, the 'Daniel Jackson takes a walk on the Dark Side'

storyline was born as a result of a contractual issue rather than a creative decision. During negotiations with Michael Shanks for season ten, Shanks was only able to do sixteen out of the twenty episodes. As a means to explain why he was gone for four episodes, Brad Wright came up with the idea to make him a Prior.

"Wouldn't Adria seek out someone just like him?" asks Wright. "Use your enemies to turn your friends? So the notion of turning Daniel into a Prior was my idea – and that's the only reason I got story credit," says the co-creator humbly. "That's kind of how it works. It's not like you sit down and type half the story, because what is a story? A story is not just the one, two, three events, it's sometimes just the key thing that sets the whole thing rolling, and so Robert generously gave me story credit."

Daniel: Jack, you have to believe me.
Jack: Why?
Daniel: Why? Well, because, oh I dunno, the fate of the galaxy hangs in the balance?
Jack: You know, that old chestnut's getting a little... old.

Equally as complimentary, Robert Cooper may have set Wright's idea into motion, but he makes sure to credit Wright with the genesis of the storyline. "Right back at the beginning of the season, Brad had said we should make one of our characters a Prior," Cooper recalls. "So Brad deserves all the credit for coming up with that idea. I took it and turned it into the arc story that it ends up being – the payoff of the search for the Sangraal."

Of course a very memorable aspect of 'The Shroud' – particularly for the established fans of the show – was the return of actor Richard Dean Anderson in the role of Major General Jack O'Neill. Though the former star and executive producer of the show had left the show in season nine, his presence, both onscreen as well as off, was always felt.

"As soon as we knew we had Rick for that episode, I knew I had to find a way to take advantage of the chemistry between him and Daniel," reveals Cooper. "They're the original two – Jackson and O'Neill. Michael and Rick have a really great way of playing off each other, so instantly you see that spark between them when they do their scenes together. It's a serious storyline but it's still funny, and that's what makes *Stargate SG-1* what it is. We've always found humor in any situation, and I think that's something which separates our series from all other science fiction shows. We don't take ourselves too seriously and we know how to tell a

Above: Adria waits
for the superweapon
to be completed.

good dramatic story but also have fun. I think that's more entertaining than always being dour, downtrodden and depressed. I love it! The interaction between O'Neill and Daniel is gold. I thought it was terrific. I was so disappointed that we were cancelled before that really got to air. Michael did such a good job in it."

Michael Shanks' portrayal of Daniel-turned-Prior was indeed applauded by both cast and crew alike – not only for his impressive acting capabilities (he steps right outside a decade-old box in 'The Shroud'), but also for his high pain threshold in the make-up chair! Å

Bounty

Written by: Damian Kindler
Directed by: Peter DeLuise

Guest Cast: Noah Danby (Cha'ra), Anne Marie DeLuise (Amy Vanderburg), David Lovgren (Darrel Grimes), Mike Dopud (Odai Ventrell), Timothy Paul Perez (Vashin), Maureen Thomas (Wendy Mitchell), Ian Robison (Frank Mitchell), Ryan Elm (Gary), Jody Thompson (Bounty Hunter), Mark Brandon (Presenter), Jeny Cassady (Alien Bounty Hunter), Brad Proctor (Alien Bounty Hunter), Jackie Blackmore (Female Grad), Ed Anders (Former Football Player), Rob Boyce (Assassin Sniper), Rob Hayter (Phil)

Mitchell rings into a cargo room and slices open a bag with his knife, finding Kassa beans inside. Sam, Teal'c and Daniel ring into similar rooms and each set C4, blowing up the Lucian Al'kesh along with four containers full of Kassa. Netan is informed and is so enraged that he places a bounty on their heads. Back on Earth, Vala persuades Mitchell to take her to his high school reunion in Kansas; Sam and Dr Lee are at a conference where they will present the chimera holographic projector; and Daniel is conducting research at a museum. Offworld, Teal'c and Cha'ra are walking through a forest when they are fired upon by staff weapons. When the shooting stops, Teal'c realizes he has been injured. Meanwhile, Daniel is asked out by an attractive woman in the museum, but when he declines, she pulls out an energy weapon and tries to shoot him. Daniel runs outside the museum, but the woman teleports in front of him and points her weapon at a woman walking down the sidewalk with her baby. Daniel surrenders, but the woman is hit by a bus. Sam begins her presentation of the chimera optics projection system, when she too is shot at, but it passes through her as she was using a holographic projection of herself. At Mitchell's high school reunion, bounty hunter Ventrell locates the Colonel at a payphone calling SGC. He pulls out a gun and, assuming Mitchell's voice, Ventrell requests assistance. Ventrell takes everyone at the reunion hostage and when SG-1 radio in, he tells them to beam in first, unarmed, and he'll let everyone go. Teal'c, Carter and Daniel appear, and Ventrell rings them all out – but only Vala, Mitchell and Ventrell disappear. The bounty hunter finds himself on the other end of SG-1's guns on the transport ship. Sam used holographic projection technology to create the illusion of their beaming into the gym. They use Ventrell to kill Netan.

Opposite: Vala is distracted by the bounty hunter.

Vala: Everybody evaluates each other's lot in life, generally by virtue of a combination of material worth and the attractiveness of one's date/spouse/life-partner. Let me go as your date?

One of the hallmarks of *Stargate SG-1* has always been its ability to produce excellent comedy episodes that still retain a more serious edge. For season ten, writer/producer Damian Kindler and long-time series director Peter DeLuise created 'Bounty', which took the classic fish-out-of-water scenario as its theme and plonked Vala in the middle of small-town America. As the writer explained to gateworld.net, however, that wasn't necessarily his original plan for the episode.

"It's a really fun Vala episode – it's a fun episode in general," he says. "I did a draft and delivered it and the guys said, 'This is great, but I think what we want to do is put Vala at Mitchell's reunion.' [That] was an idea that had been bandied around before when I was talking about the script initially. It didn't gel at that point but it gelled once the script came in. So I said, 'You know what? That's great!' Never had such a big note been delivered to me and had been accepted by me so happily. It was like, 'No, I don't mind doing it! I'll totally make that work.'"

'Bounty' thus became yet another example of how well the collaborative process employed by the writing team really works. Once Kindler had found a way of incorporating the idea of Vala accompanying Mitchell into his original script, he reports that it was a cinch to meld the two elements together.

Below: "They're worth how much?"

"Once the second pass came in everyone was very happy with it because that was a wonderful dynamic," recalls the writer. "That's perfect. Let's put Vala in small-town Kansas with aliens after them. And it's great! Her character, when used properly, is just absolutely wonderful grist for the mill on *SG-1*. So I really loved what she brought to the show."

Director Peter DeLuise also brought his own distinctive input to the show – both behind

and in front of the camera. There has been a long history of DeLuise family members appearing in *Stargate SG-1* and 'Bounty' was no exception, since the character of Amy Vanderberg, Mitchell's high school crush, was played by actress Anne Marie Loder, who also happens to be DeLuise's wife!

Above: Ventrell (Mike Dopud) makes his point.

Ventrell: Name's Ventrell. I'm here to collect the price on your head.

There were also a few comedy 'asides' that Kindler and DeLuise put in for eagle-eyed fans. For example, the posters on the wall outside Mitchell's old school auditorium feature both the writer running for 'Class Treasurer' and the director running for 'Class Secretary'. Who says you can't have fun whilst shooting on a television schedule?

"'Bounty' was fun," agrees star Ben Browder, who got to explore more of Mitchell's backstory as the character realised that he may never be able to leave his SGC persona behind. "Claudia was just hysterical – you take Vala's character into that environment, and all Mitchell can do is stand there and go, 'Oh, no, I knew I shouldn't have brought her... I tried to talk her out of it... What was I thinking?' But that's fun stuff as well – [there were] some good Vala and Mitchell comedy moments." Å

Bad Guys

Written by: Martin Gero	Guest Cast: Sean Allan (Chancellor), Danielle
Directed by: Peter DeLuise	Kremeniuk (Hesellven), Haley Beauchamp (Sylvana),
Story by: Martin Gero,	Brent O'Connor (Heron), Joshua Malina (Cicero), Alistair
Ben Browder	Abell (Jayem Saran), Ron Canada (Quartus), Richard
	Zeman (Lourdes)

SG-1 minus Carter (who is in Washington with the President) go in search of the planet P4M-328 to find the Clava Thessara Infinitas. Arriving on the planet, they discover that they are actually inside a museum which happens to be hosting a party. It is a first contact situation and according to protocol, when a civilization reaches a certain level of development, SG-1 have to send the MALP to make contact before they do it in person. As Mitchell pushes the glyphs on the DHD to return home, he realizes that it is plastic – it's a replica model of a DHD. The team have to wait for their scheduled check-in with General Landry in just under six hours. Before then, however, they are discovered in the museum and mistaken for rebels by a group of party-goers attending the museum's function. The team rapidly realize that trying to explain that they are explorers isn't going to work, and so they decide to go with the rebel cover until they can extricate themselves from the situation. Unfortunately the authorities who arrived to handle the 'rebel situation' lock them in with some of the party-goers. One was injured and a medical team arrives to assist, attempting to end the situation inside the museum by launching an attack on SG-1, during which Daniel is stunned. Cicero, one of the museum's curators, believes their story and decides to help, telling them how to appear more like the rebels they are impersonating. He shows them some of the institution's artifacts, including a Goa'uld Naquadah bomb, housed inside a case. Thinking it could be useful, Vala tries to reach it and triggers a lockdown on the Naquadah bomb. Knowing it can't be deactivated, Mitchell and Vala use the bomb to dial out. SG-1 are then captured by Quartus' military forces but Mitchell convinces him to let them travel home through the gate, assuring him that whilst some races may intend his people harm, SG-1 most certainly do not.

Daniel: Look, there's been a terrible misunderstanding. You see, we're not rebels.

The initial idea for 'Bad Guys' came directly from series star Ben Browder, and was so catchy that it stuck: specifically in the head of writer/producer Martin Gero.

"Ben had come up with this great idea that we go to a museum. There's some sort of function there, we get stuck and they think we're terrorists... the bad guys. I really liked the idea and Ben didn't have any time to write it, being the lead in a television show," Gero quips. "I came up with the *Die Hard* idea on top, so I wrote an outline and I showed it to Rob who really liked it."

"Basically I said, 'I think it's kind of interesting: we walk in to these places toting guns where people haven't seen anybody like this before and they kind of go, "Oh, hello, soldiers!"'" explains Browder, of where his initial idea came from. "What if we walked into the Metropolitan Museum of Art carrying guns and then said, 'We're aliens from another planet'? What is George Bush going to say? That was my basic precept – for a minute, let's be realistic about this. These people come through a hoop and say they're aliens from a distant planet, and they're carrying weapons! One, we're going to take the weapons away if we can. Two, we're going to lock them away for a very long time and get them some help!"

Above: A civilian thinks he's saving the day.

Browder is no stranger to the writing craft, having penned several scripts for *Farscape* during his time as a lead on that show. However, he is quick to play down his involvement in the writing of 'Bad Guys', and very anxious about giving credit where he feels it is most due.

"Coop [Robert Cooper] and I had a long discussion about whether I should take credit or not," Browder says frankly. "Martin decided he liked the idea, so we talked a little bit about it and he went and did the whole script and showed me and I made a few comments. That was pretty much it. It was [a] story and, you know, scripts are about the execution – not only in the writing but the directing, the acting, the editing... The credit duly goes to Martin for that script, not me. Actors sometimes have a history of going 'Yeah, that was my idea!' I'm vaguely uncomfortable with that. Well, everybody's got an idea! Why would you take credit for it? I mean, a good idea is a good idea; it doesn't matter where it comes from. The execution of it, that's the work."

When it came to actually writing the script, Gero found it particularly enjoyable. Having consulted on the many *Stargate SG-1* episodes that have gone before the camera since the writer joined the staff, 'Bad Guys' was actually only the second he'd had the chance to write.

"I really enjoyed writing 'The Powers That Be' for season nine," Gero says of his first foray into the *Stargate SG-1* universe, "but I never really felt like that was my *SG-1* episode because I had to write it before Rob had written any of the Ori stuff. So I essentially wrote the first three acts and the rest had to essentially be rewritten, but I was too busy to do it because I was working on *Stargate: Atlantis*. So this was the first one that I did from end to end. 'Bad Guys' suited my sensibilities. I really enjoyed it."

Mitchell: We got ourselves a bit of a John McClane here.
Jackson: What? What are you talking about?
Teal'c: *Die Hard.*

Another memorable aspect of 'Bad Guys' was the museum setting in which the team accidentally find themselves. Filmed on location in a school in Vancouver, production designer James Robbins and the set decoration department had great fun revisiting the show's past to provide the elaborate museum displays.

"Oh, man!" laughs Robbins, recalling the task. "You know what, I don't think any other show could have achieved that. We had ten years of collecting Egyptian paraphernalia and the size of the actual set decoration lock-ups that we have on this show [are huge]. I think they brought, like, four or five tons [of items]. We emptied the lock-ups! Anything Egyptian was in there. They went through and placed everything. I was down there every day for three or four days, picking where things were going to go."

Shooting on location meant that some of the beats the script called for were quite difficult to perform on set. To accommodate those story elements, Robbins worked with Michelle Comens in the visual effects department to put all the elements together.

"We had specific gags that we had to make sure were in there, like when they shot out the case and the bars dropped down," the designer

Above: Vala figures out a way home.

explains. "Of course, we shot that in an actual school, so there's nowhere for those bars to come from. What we did was put up a black tape line on the ceiling and installed the bars physically. Visual effects locked the camera off to shoot an angle, we put the bars in and visual effects do the moment or two where they slam down and they appear to come out of the hole that is actually just a tape line on the ceiling. Then [there was] the window where Vala does all of her sneakiness trying to get the Goa'uld arc bomb out, so I had to play a bunch of gags for her cutting the glass. We also built the interior pyramid set that they were fooled by, thinking that it was an actual pyramid they had gated into. That was fun – I intentionally didn't make conventional treatments, I made them look like facades, so that they start to realize that things aren't quite right, things like light switches on the walls and stuff like that. It was amazing."

"I think the episode turned out pretty good," says Martin Gero. "It was really long – about fourteen minutes over. There was some stuff taken out, but I think for the most part it turned out pretty good. At the end of the day, I always think the quicker an episode can go the better, I prefer to overwrite a little bit and then cut it back." Å

Talion

Written by: Damian Kindler Directed by: Andy Mikita	Guest Cast: Lexa Doig (Dr Carolyn Lam), Tony Amendola (Bra'tac), Craig Fairbrass (Arkad), Peter Kent (Ba'kal), John Tench (Lizan), Aaron Brooks (Nisal)

Teal'c and Bra'tac are caught in the carnage when a meeting of the Jaffa Council is attacked, and SG-1 bring them both back to the SGC. Teal'c wakes after two weeks, but Bra'tac, who was more severely hurt, remains in a coma. Teal'c discovers that they were attacked by Ba'kal, a Jaffa working for Arkad, who wants to follow the Ori. Landry does not want to commit the SGC to an investigation, so Teal'c decides to leave alone, refusing SG-1's help. When he wakes, a still-sick Bra'tac tells Daniel that Arkad murdered Teal'c's mother, though he could not avenge her death at the time since he was still First Prime. Teal'c catches up with Ba'kal, killing the Jaffa when he won't give up any information, but soon afterwards Arkad contacts the SGC, asking to discuss the situation and promising to halt a planned attack on Earth. He blames another Jaffa faction for the attack on the Jaffa Council, and vows to take them out. He warns Earth to stay out of the way – perhaps in the future they will become allies once more, although Arkad still plans to convert to Origin. Landry orders SG-1 to find Teal'c, as his actions could interfere with Earth's fragile negotiations. They are told to use any means necessary, even if it means firing on their friend. SG-1 and SG-3 arrive at Arkad's pyramid base ahead of Teal'c, intending to capture him, but Teal'c renders SG-3 unconscious and fires on Mitchell when the Colonel gets in his way. He's determined to avenge his mother and the Jaffa Council. Ignoring Daniel's pleas, Teal'c stuns all but Mitchell, who briefly manages to fight Teal'c before he too is knocked out. Teal'c continues towards Arkad's pyramid, but Arkad's guards capture him. Arkad offers to fight Teal'c with a staff weapon, and proceeds to best Teal'c, taunting him. Hearing Arkad boast about killing his mother is too much for Teal'c, who pulls out a final burst of energy and impales Arkad on a metal spike. Later, back at the SGC, SG-1 falsify a report to Landry which says they were held prisoner and rescued by Teal'c.

Daniel (to Arkad): Bra'tac sends his regards as well. I don't think he'll mind me speaking for him when I say that he'd love to stab you in the eye with a really big knife.

'Talion' will always hold a special place in director Andy Mikita's heart, as it signified the final time he would be stepping behind the camera to bring an episode of *Stargate SG-1* to life. Having been with the show from the very beginning, Mikita confesses that the end of his time on the series was a tough thing to contemplate.

"It was an emotional episode for me," he says. "I was so happy that it was a story about Chris. They have all become very dear and close friends of mine, but Chris certainly has a special place in everyone's heart. He's just a big teddy bear of a guy and we go on golf trips together all the time and he's a very dear friend, and it was an honor to work with him on that episode."

"That was the last episode that I was actually heavy in for the season," recalls Judge, "and for me it represented a lot of closure. Not only [because it] got back to truly who Teal'c was, but it was directed by Andy Mikita, who was a first assistant director on the pilot. It was just really wonderful to do my last episode where Teal'c was the A-story with Andy. For me that was the one that really stuck out."

Above: Teal'c is unstoppable.

When Judge says it was "Teal'c heavy", he's certainly not kidding. 'Talion' featured some of the most spectacular stunts of the season – and the director is swift to point out that Judge was right in the forefront of those scenes.

"He really invested himself in that episode," Mikita recalls. "I don't think I've ever seen anyone work so hard on an episode of TV as Chris did. He got really into it. All those fight sequences, that was really him. We had a stunt double that we put in from time to time, but the lion's share of that was definitely Chris. He took a beating," the director laughs. "He had to get stitched up over one eye at one point when they were rehearsing the fight."

"I wanted the fights to be big," Judge explains with a laugh. "The bad thing was that we were rehearsing the fight stuff after we were shooting the previous episode, so I was a little tired. I bobbed when I should have weaved and one of the stunt guys caught me in the forehead and gave me a nice big gash!"

Despite the collective enthusiasm on set during the filming of the episode, the shoot and subsequent post-production period wasn't without its problems. For a start, the special effects department created a wonderful pyrotechnic sequence which went wrong at the last minute.

"We did a big explosion shot where I put a camera overhead on a big construction crane," Mikita explains. "A big fireball came up and engulfed the camera. It was a film camera and we had it wrapped in nomex [fire resistant material], but the flames completely engulfed the camera and the entire camera just burst into flames. We're all standing there watching this great shot – it looked really cool having this huge fireball go right up into the camera – but it lit it on fire."

Mikita and the crew feared the worst – the fire hadn't just licked the camera, it had completely enveloped the rig. They were convinced that both the camera and the film they had shot was destroyed. "We brought the camera down," continues Mikita, "and it was just a big black lump of charcoal. We pulled all the nomex off it and eventually managed to get the film out. We sent it off to the lab, and it ended up being fine! That's the shot we use in the episode!"

Ba'kal: Where are you going?
Teal'c: I am leaving. You are about to explode.

Another problem was that the episode ran extremely long, forcing Mikita to hack down a lot of material that he would have preferred to keep in his final edit.

"We had to cut ten or twelve minutes from the show as we went so over," he explains. "It's nice to have maybe five minutes to cut, but anything over ten minutes and you're losing a day of shooting and usually full scenes have to be taken away. That was certainly the case in 'Talion'. There was a whole fight sequence we had to cut of the antagonist under Bra'tac's leadership when he was younger, and he killed his opponent in a training session under Bra'tac's tutorship. It was a shame that we had to take out so much of the episode, and we kind of knew we were going to. We do a preliminary estimated timing and those estimates came in quite long – about fifty-five minutes. I traditionally tend to shoot a little bit long, so I was concerned that they chose to leave the script at that length.

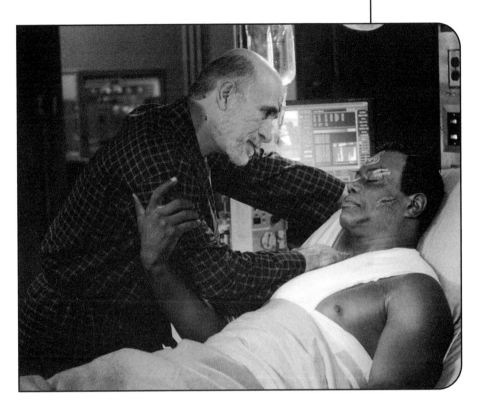

We shot it as it was, and there was a lot of stuff that had to go."

Mikita also had to drop a particular scene that was very dear to his heart, as he explains: "At the end, there's the big fight sequence and I missed a shot that I knew we had to get. I had the plug pulled on me because we had gone into overtime. It was a very important shot of when he gets impaled on the weapon rack, so I ended up having to go back and doing that another time with a double, and I couldn't shoot the guy's face. You wouldn't notice, but for me it was a big deal and I was personally offended by that because it was my last *SG-1* shot ever, and I couldn't do it," he laughs, remembering his chagrin. "It bugged me terribly at the time, but in the end, it wasn't really that big of a deal.

"I was pretty happy with it," Mikita concludes of the episode. "I think it turned out well. It looked better with all the deleted scenes in it, but there's nothing you can do about it – it has to be on time, so things had to be sacrificed as a result. But Chris did a great job and it was so much fun to be working with him. He deserved and earned that episode." Å

Above: A lucky Teal'c recovers back at the SGC.

Family Ties

Written by: Joseph Mallozzi & Paul Mullie

Directed by: Peter DeLuise

Guest Cast: Fred Willard (Jacek), Lexa Doig (Dr Carolyn Lam), Dan Shea (Sergeant Siler), Fulvio Cecere (Colonel Davidson), Robin Richardson (Trader), Doreen Ramus (Hazel), Lillianne Lee (Kim), Paul Wu (De'vir)

Vala's shopping trip with Carter is curtailed by the arrival of her estranged father, Jacek, offering information on a planned attack on Earth by Arkad. SG-1 agrees to meet him, but Vala is suspicious. An initial scout seems to indicate that Jacek was being truthful, so Landry authorizes his visit to Earth. Three weeks go by, but Vala refuses to talk to her father. Landry, who is trying to establish contact with his ex-wife, offers her some advice – don't let the opportunity to patch up past family difficulties go by. Vala tries, but her father attempts to buy her affections with a necklace and is then caught selling 'authentic stardust' on the Internet. Worse still, she and Daniel discover that he is in contact with a group of Jaffa, Arkad's advance team, hidden in a cloaked ship already on Earth. Jacek reveals they were having second thoughts so he had offered to find a buyer for their naquadah for a split of the profits. He knows how to calibrate SGC's sensors to locate the Jaffa ship, and works with Sam to do so – asking her to dinner, unsuccessfully, in the process. They find the ship, but Jacek says it is rigged to explode if moved, although he has the deactivation code. He asks Landry for one more chance to prove himself, and the general agrees, sending Vala with him. Jacek tries to pass Vala off as his partner, but the Jaffa are suspicious and SG-1 have to step in. Vala saves her father's life, and he says he doesn't want to risk her life whilst disarming the ship's self-destruct. He takes off, admitting via radio that the ship was never really rigged – he just wanted the naquadah. But SG-1 already knew this, and replaced the ship with a fake, which is what Jacek has escaped in. His buyer isn't best pleased, but of course Vala's father finds a way out of his tight spot. Back on Earth, Vala and Carter prepare for a girl's night in, and Teal'c goes to the theatre, courtesy of Jacek...

Opposite: Vala is less than thrilled to see her dad.

Jacek: I suppose for the benefit of your friends there, you're going to want to list all the reasons I was such a bad father?

Vala: Oh I wish I could, but a wormhole can only be maintained for thirty-eight minutes.

When they came up with the idea for 'Family Ties', writers Joseph Mallozzi and Paul Mullie didn't know that it would be the last script for *Stargate SG-1* they would ever write. That didn't stop them taking full of advantage of the fact, however!

"We knew what the story was going to be before we knew it was going to be our last one for the show," explains Mallozzi. "So we went in with that story, had fun with it, and took some shots at the network. It was a lot of fun to write. It was the last script we would ever write for *SG-1*, and we had some not-so-thinly veiled shots at the network for the cancellation!"

"There were more in the first draft," adds Paul Mullie. "[But] to me, that was nothing compared to the ending. The couple of shots we took at the network were fine, but the fact that we got away with that ending – that was what made that a great final episode for us."

Before they got to the ending, though, the writers had a lot of other elements to juggle. With the end of the season imminent, they took the opportunity to open up some of the characters that viewers hadn't really had a chance to get to know.

"It was nice to focus on some Vala backstory," Mallozzi pinpoints specifically. "We all knew about her past as a Gou'ald, but we knew nothing of her as a human being. While we were doing that, it gave us the opportunity to parallel that with Landry and his relationship with his family."

Daniel [about Vala]: You want us to talk to her for you?
Jacek: I was going to suggest tricking her into coming here, but if you think talking will work...

Exploring Vala's family meant introducing her estranged father, played by Fred Willard, an esteemed comic actor and star of movies such as *Anchorman: The Legend of Ron Burgundy*, in which he played Ed Harken. Willard was a perfect match for actress Claudia Black, and Mallozzi and Mullie were delighted that he pulled off the character they had created for him so perfectly.

"He was awesome," recalls Mallozzi. "In the past, certain guest stars haven't worked out. You write a character and the individual guest star comes in and doesn't really deliver. But in this case, we actually wrote the character for Fred Willard. He agreed to do the episode, so we wrote it for him, and he did such a terrific job. He improvised a bunch of stuff that we kept in."

Besides the little digs at the network for cancelling their show, Mallozzi

Above: Jacek (Fred Willard) tries out his best lines on Carter.

and Mullie also managed to get a few other gags in there – in particular, as Mullie alluded to previously, the hilarious final scene in which Teal'c attends a performance of something called *The Virginia Monologues*.

"We kept expecting someone to take it out," Mallozzi confesses, of the *Vagina Monologues* pastiche.

"Nobody said we had to," Mullie explains, "including the network, so we just left it in! We did have to change it, because originally it was the actual *Vagina Monologues*."

"They said, 'As much as we love [it], the fact that we're on *Stargate* means you can't use the exact wording,'" Mallozzi agrees. "Originally, it was an actual script from the *Vagina Monologues*, but we had to come up with alternate dialogue. I can't remember who, but someone said, 'I don't think I've ever heard the word vagina used so many times in thirty seconds!'"

"Chris was just great," concludes Mullie, of how the final scene turned out, "and the people sitting beside him in the theatre were people who work on the show – so keep your eyes peeled!" Å

Dominion

Story by: Alex Levine	Guest Cast: Peter Flemming (Malcolm Barrett),
Teleplay by: Alan McCullough	Jonathan Walker (Ta'seem)
Directed by: William Waring	

SG-1 implant Vala with false memories of the whereabouts of the clava thessara infinatus in a plan to lure Adria into an ambush. Because Vala believes that these memories are real, so too does Adria. As they go in search of the key, SG-1 show up with an anti-Prior device to prevent Adria from using her powers. Just as they are about to take action however, SG-1 are surrounded by Jaffa, who proceed to kidnap Adria and beam her onboard Ba'al's ship. Ba'al keeps Adria in a prison which disables her powers, and he reveals that he is going to take control of the Ori armies by implanting Adria with a symbiote. Finally, SG-1 locate the ship and beam Adria back to the *Odyssey*, but it's not Adria as they know her – Ba'al is now in her body. By taking on a more powerful host, he can now command the Ori army. Teal'c wants to kill Adria and Ba'al, but there is no guarantee that the Ori army would cease fighting, even if Adria were dead. SG-1 need to swap Ba'al's symbiote for someone they can trust, and they decide on the Tok'ra – a species who want to stop the Ori just as much as they do. But on hearing their plan, Ba'al tells SG-1 that he will kill Adria the moment they try to remove him. The Tok'ra contingent arrives, but the extraction procedure that they are about to undertake is extremely difficult. Even though they have refined the process considerably, there remains a real risk that Adria will not survive. Adria is zapped unconscious, and the Tok'ra symbiote is surgically placed inside her. During the surgery, they are able to extract Ba'al, but he releases a deadly toxin into Adria's nervous system. The Tok'ra symbiote can't heal her, and the host is too weak for the proceedure to take effect. Knowing that she is going to die, Adria locks herself in the infirmary with Vala and completes her ascension.

Adria: You've made a terrible mistake. Release me now and I will be merciful.

Ba'al: You're so much more pleasant when you lack the ability to snap my neck with your thoughts.

"For whatever reason, this episode was easy to write," shares 'Dominion' writer, Alan McCullough. "I don't know why, but some episodes are really difficult to write and some episodes are easier. 'Dominion' just all came together very nicely."

The idea for the penultimate episode of Stargate SG-1's tenth season was thought up by Alex Levine – the show's script coordinator. With the original germ for the episode revolving around the subtext 'How do SG-1 capture Adria?' it was Levine who pitched the concept of the memory trick. It was this gimmick which enabled a telekinetic Adria to fall into the hands of SG-1 (before getting snatched out again), allowing the storyline to progress the way the writers and directors had hoped.

"That was a great idea," praises McCullough. "It worked so well because entirely separately I had pitched out a standalone story where a Prior gets infected with a Goa'uld symbiote which gives him Goa'uld powers. Robert [Cooper] and I were talking about it, and we discussed that Priors weren't as interesting as Adria.

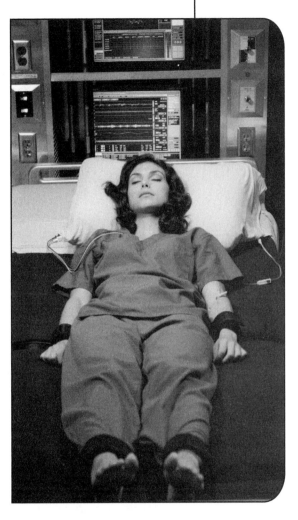

Above: *Is this really the end of Adria?*

Somewhere along the line, we decided to put those two stories together and we ended up with 'Dominion'. I think one of the reasons it was so easy to write is that the plot was so dense. It moved so quickly that you didn't have to spend a lot of time in one place, you didn't have to stretch the dialogue – it was just scene, scene, scene."

Because they knew the series was coming to an end, the main marching orders for 'Dominion' were that it had to wrap up the Adria/Vala storyline, deal with Ba'al, leave the option open for new things down the road, confirm that the Ori were dead, and pave the way for what eventually became the first movie, *The Ark of Truth*.

"That was the challenge, figuring out a way to do all of that," laughs McCullough. "Writing Ba'al inside Adria was... interesting, for sure. Ultimately you're just writing Ba'al, but you have to hope that it won't sound weird coming out of Morena's mouth – which it didn't. She did a great job with it. That was something we were wrestling with – how do we make this believable?"

The task of killing off season ten's big baddie was a bittersweet moment for the relatively new *Stargate SG-1* writer. Not only was McCullough faced with the daunting task of wrapping up all the loose ends, but this episode was going to be the last *Stargate SG-1* episode that he would write.

"It was sad," admits McCullough, "but I've subsequently been rehired on *Stargate: Atlantis*. That wasn't guaranteed when I was writing 'Dominion' and we knew there was going to be some downsizing of the writing staff. I thought that maybe my time with *Stargate* was coming to an end, so it was definitely bittersweet. Ultimately now I'm on *Stargate: Atlantis*, and it's great to be working on that show with so many of the same people behind the scenes."

Landry: Ba'al is in Adria?
Mitchell: Yes, sir. It's the bad-guy equivalent of cordon bleu.

Just as it was the last episode for McCullough, so too was it the final one for long-standing director Will Waring. Popular amongst cast and crew, Waring was admittedly apprehensive about the episode.

"I was definitely not looking forward to finishing shooting 'Dominion', but at the time, I kind of thought we'd be doing the films, so I knew I'd see these guys again. They've become good friends.

"'Dominion' was a really fun episode though," continues Waring. "It's always great shooting with Morena [Baccarin] – she's a hoot."

The other guest actor in that episode that Waring enjoys working with is Ba'al's Cliff Simon. A man who has caused trouble for SG-1 for a number of years, Ba'al's demise had to be a memorable and dramatic moment in *Stargate SG-1*'s ten-year history.

"I wanted a good death for Ba'al," shares Waring, "so we squibbed him up front and back. A squib is a tiny explosive charge that we put in an outfit. The wardrobe is slightly scored and underneath a heavy leather or metal chest-plate is worn, and there is a small explosive charge on it with a blood pack. It's got wires going down the pant legs and out to a

firing box, which is remote controlled, wirelessly, so at the right moment
you hit the button and all these squibs explode. If it works, blood shoots
out all across the set, and if it's backlit, then you over-crank the camera
to slow it all down a little bit. That way you can get all these geysers of
blood shooting out of the chest and out of the back as you get shot.

*Above: Invasion of
the Body Snatcher.*

"In this episode I also had Mitchell with the big machine gun, the
G36, which is a big gun, unload a full clip into Ba'al as he's running
forward," Waring continues with relish. "It's pretty dramatic, but it's fun
to do because usually the deaths in *Stargate* are smaller than that. We
wanted to make sure we saw a good death for Cliff. And he's the kind of
guy that loves to wear the squibs, so he had a great time dying!"

But this is science fiction – and that means no one really dies. SG-1
soon discover that the Ba'al they thought they killed may just have been
another one of his clones. So have we really seen the last of the evil
System Lord?

"You'll just have to watch the films to find out," smiles Waring. Å

Unending

Story by: Robert C. Cooper
Directed by: Robert C. Cooper

Guest Cast: Bruce Woloshyn (Gate Guard)

The Asgard invite Stargate Command to their homeworld to give them important news. Thor announces that a number of Asgard are waiting to beam aboard the *Odyssey* to begin installing technological upgrades on their ship. The Asgard are planning on giving SG-1 all of their technology and all of their knowledge as their race are dying out. As the final installations are completed, three Ori motherships exit hyperspace and attack the *Odyssey*. General Landry orders that they use the new weapons on the Ori mothership, and they succeed in destroying it. But more Ori battlecruisers arrive – they are tracking the Asgard's system. The *Odyssey* heads for the nearest planet with a Stargate and offloads the crew. SG-1 and Landry stay onboard and the *Odyssey* is attacked. With an incoming blast from an Ori ship, Carter activates an Asgard time-dilation field and the Ori blast freezes. While time may appear to be passing at a normal rate for the team, years will pass inside the bubble, while mere fractions of a second pass outside the field. Carter plans to make the necessary modifications to the *Odyssey* so they can take it out of phase without the blast hitting them – but she is unable to come up with a solution. The weeks onboard turn into months and then into years. During those years, Daniel and Vala fall in love, Carter learns to play the cello, Landry develops a gardening hobby, Mitchell grows increasingly angry, and Teal'c changes very little – his long Jaffa lifespan means that he ages far more slowly than the others. Fifty years later, with Landry having passed away and SG-1 (apart from Teal'c) very elderly, Sam figures out how to reverse time within a localized field – using the Ori energy beam to provide the power. But one member of the team will have to remain old and retain the memories so that they don't repeat history. Teal'c volunteers as he has many more years to live. The plan works, and back home SG-1 try to get Teal'c to divulge what happened on the ship – but he remains tight-lipped. With their next mission awaiting them, Daniel, Vala, Carter, Mitchell, and Teal'c step through the Stargate once more.

Mitchell: When I said that I wanted to get the team back together, work with you guys, learn from you... I did not mean every waking moment for the next fifty years.
Daniel: You said that yesterday.

Executive producer Robert C. Cooper took up the daunting challenge of both writing and directing the final episode for *Stargate SG-1*'s concluding season in its present television run. Anticipating a renewal for an eleventh season, Cooper originally planned to end season ten with a cliff-hanger finale. But when the show's cancellation was announced in August 2006, the writers had to come up with a suitable ending for *Stargate SG-1*.

Having faced a similar problem when the show's five-year run on Showtime finished at the end of season five, the writers and producers were adamant that they would leave the door open for more *SG-1* adventures.

"'Unending' came from a phone call which told us that we didn't have much time left to wrap the series up," explains Cooper. "Sci Fi wanted us to put a cap on the whole thing and I had written a two-part story that I had planned to end season ten with – it was a cliff-hanger. Obviously that wouldn't do. They didn't want us putting 'to be continued' on the last episode."

Above: *Daniel and Vala find true love.*

Whilst there was no certain end to SG-1's adventures, Cooper thought it was important to have some sort of closure out of respect for the fans. It was an end without an end, if you will – hence the title of the episode.

"We felt that we owed the fans some sort of goodbye, and that's why when we came up with the story of 'Unending'," Cooper explains. "There was always the intention to have SG-1's adventures continue. We were never going to blow up the SGC and kill everybody. There was always going to be some sort of resolution, but then we wanted it all to continue so that the fan fiction can live on. We liked the idea that we would get the chance to encapsulate our heroes' lives and see one version of the future that they might live out.

"What everyone always talked about on this show was the team. They loved the episodes when the team was together. When you asked fans, 'If you could have one episode that you could chose for us to write, what elements would you want?' at the top of the list would be, 'We want the team to be together.' To me, the answer was, 'Okay, you want the team to be together? We'll make them together... alone... for a long time.' This provided us with the opportunity to have some really dramatic, wonderful moments between these people, some of whom have already lived a decade together in real life."

Having the team spend over fifty years on a ship together acted as an emotional tribute to all ten seasons which came before 'Unending'. Surely the weight of ending the series must have been a heavy one to bear?

"There was a lot of stress involved," laughs Cooper good-naturedly. "I wanted to live up to what I knew the expectations would be. People have invested a lot of emotion and time and feel very strongly about the show, and you can never really do that justice, you can never really satisfy that level of fandom, so you have to set this aside and say, 'I have forty-five minutes to make some entertainment.'

Mitchell [about the Stargate]: That is how we are supposed to travel millions of light years across the galaxy to other planets.

"It was important to me that I didn't overstep my boundaries as a director and didn't make the show overly stylized to the point of drawing attention to the directing," Cooper says. "I wanted the directing in that particular case to just showcase the actors and the performances. I think the episode has a lot of emotional impact, especially at the end when they're all going through the gate for the last time on the show. I told the production that no matter what happened, I wanted the last shot to be of the team going through the gate. I did it as much for the actors – as a tribute for them – as it was important for the show. It was a special moment to wind that all up at 2am with the last shot at the gate. Everybody was really choked up about it. It is something that I will always be very proud to have been a part of. It was a privilege for me."

Cooper's efforts to make sure that the actors also had a sense of closure was met with great appreciation from the cast and crew alike. *Stargate SG-1* had been a huge part of all their lives – whether it had been for ten years or ten months.

With 'Unending' being the last episode of the television series, some of

the cast invented B-stories for their characters during their time on the *Odyssey*. Two such people were Amanda Tapping and Christopher Judge, who both decided that there was more to their story than first meets the eye.

Above: *Mitchell looks more like Carter every day.*

"Christopher and I had all this stuff that we were trying to say subtly between Teal'c and Carter. In our reality, they got together. We made it very subtle, but there are little hints – at the table they are holding hands for example – it's just little things that we did for ourselves and we didn't want to go over the top. It doesn't translate onscreen necessarily, but if you look for it, you'll see it in moments. Maybe you won't pick up on it, but for us, it made sense that the friendship had evolved."

Carter and Teal'c's relationship has certainly evolved since the show began in 1997. And theirs is one of many. Friends, families and lovers have come and gone, but when one gate closes, another surely opens. With an endless possibility of worlds and alternate realities to visit, *Stargate SG-1* has many more chevrons to explore. Actor Ben Browder refers to the show as "the vampire which never dies", and let's hope that he's right.

"When asked the question, 'How do you want to see the show end?'" ponders Michael Shanks, "I have always said, 'I just want to see the team go out through that gate one more time and that's where they can live – in the audience's imagination.' I think that was the best thing that we did in the last episode – having the team go off for more adventures. I don't think you can end this show completely and just say, 'That's it! You can all go home!' We want to live on, we want to carry on those dreams and adventures in the imagination of our fans and in our own imaginations also." Å

All these writers, and they couldn't come up with something better?

Stargate SG-1 has officially entered the television record books. It is now the longest-running, scripted, made-for-cable television series in US broadcasting history. Airing in over 120 countries, dubbed and subtitled in multiple languages, and with a franchise that has spawned numerous novels, computer games, action figures and more, *Stargate SG-1* is unquestionably a worldwide success.

As a science fiction show, *Stargate SG-1* often has to take its themes and situations pretty seriously if it's to expect the same of the audience. But every so often, the cast and crew allow the viewers a sneak peak of the sub-rosa humor which brims behind the scenes. And what better way to celebrate *Stargate SG-1's* two hundredth birthday than with two hundred laughs.

The seminal episode is a collaborative effort penned by a team of the show's seven writers. An homage to fans of every stripe, '200' comments on the contrariness of TV, and of science fiction TV in particular

"'200' was fun, but scary as hell!" laughs Brad Wright. "Robert had the original idea that we should all do it – mainly because he didn't want to have to arm-wrestle for it."

When Robert Cooper announced to his band of merry writers that he wanted them all to write the two hundredth episode with a structure akin to *The Simpsons'* 'Treehouse of Horror' episodes, they thought he was joking. He wanted a 'remember when' episode where SG-1 would reminisce about past adventures and adventures that they went on that we hadn't seen before.

"It was a group effort," explains Cooper. "It was a blast. I didn't originally want to do anything that special for the show. I just thought we'd have a big party and make a big deal of it behind the scenes, but I wasn't going to make too much of the episode. And then it came down to who was going to write it, and that's when I had the brainstorm that we should all write it. We had always kicked around little ideas in the writers' room. Everybody would pitch stupid things that would never make it into a normal episode just because it was funny in the room to talk about it, and so I thought, 'Well, why not do those things? Why not put those in an episode?' It became what I imagine to be like working on a show like *Saturday Night Live* – it's a sketch comedy where you're all sitting around pitching your sketch for the show

and then you go away and write it. Everybody turned in their section and I strung it all together and tried to make it work."

The landmark outing brings back Willie Garson as Martin Lloyd, who was last seen in the show's one hundredth episode, 'Wormhole X-Treme!'. Lloyd's return to SGC is the premise which allows the cast and crew to break outside the mould of the traditional *Stargate SG-1* episode while revisiting a comical storyline from one hundred episodes ago.

"The one thing that really made the show was the brainstorm to have it be a script that Martin Lloyd had written," shares Cooper. "Originally it was just these crazy ideas – the *Wizard of Oz*, the puppets, invisible O'Neill, etc. Having a glue that had it still exist in the *Stargate* universe with our real characters was really important."

Whilst Cooper is pleased with how the one hundredth episode, 'Wormwhole X-Treme!', turned out, he does admit to a flaw in the main story: it wasn't about SG-1.

"I wanted to make sure '200' was a celebration of our team, so having our guys sitting around a table and then for them to transpose into the world of the script that Marty had put together was what made all that other stuff really work. It was the dramatic excuse to have that much fun and I don't care what other people think – whether it wasn't *Stargate*, or whatever – every hundred episodes or so, I think we're entitled to make

Above: Martin Lloyd's actors look the part.

Above: They're off to
see the Wizard.

one for ourselves. Clearly someone else thought it was pretty good too, as the episode was nominated for a Hugo Award.

"It was also a bit of a love-letter to the fans," continues Cooper. "It was all those moments that fans had chatted about. There were some digs and we made fun of ourselves. Everybody got shots taken at them, and we had some fun with some of the fan things, like the Furlings. We also made fun of some of the sillier sci-fi conceits that we fall into – the traps that we end up having to deal with on a daily basis on the show, like always beaming out of situations. That damn Asgard beam… I'm sorry we ever invented that," he laughs.

Making fun of themselves is something that the *Stargate SG-1* crew do better than most. The forty-five minute episode includes a *Star Trek* parody, a shout-out to *Farscape*, a hilarious look-see at a possible *Teal'c P.I.*, a *Wizard of Oz* sketch, a zombie action sequence, a *Dawson's Creek*-style soap, *Team America* puppets, and a host of other references thrown in for good measure. The plot of '200' is merely a device for self-mockery and enables the show's producers to bring back familiar faces into a legion of in-jokes and playful genre parodies which spares no one in the cast.

Whilst he's at the SGC, Martin Lloyd finds out that his starring actor has dropped out of the film. "How am I supposed to tell the story without my

Above: Daniel gets to grips with a Furling.

lead actor?" he asks. "Easy, just bring in a character to replace him," says Browder, who joined the show after Richard Dean Anderson's departure.

And after a one-year hiatus, Anderson returned to *Stargate SG-1* for '200', much to the delight of the show's fans.

Unsure of whether Anderson was going to be able to be in the two hundredth episode, the writers penned most of the ideas in the episode to work without him. This was the germ for the invisible O'Neill skit. Director Martin Wood suggested that the invisible O'Neill come down a hall, carrying a visible coffee cup. It would require an actor in a special green suit that would allow him to be removed later using special effects.

"We started talking about how to shoot that and that we needed to get a guy in a green suit," explains Cooper. "And then for some reason in the production meeting we realised that we didn't have a 'guy in a green suit' but that Rick was there that day and he was going to do the scene anyway. So, as it turned out, it was Rick in the green suit... even though you can't see him."

It's obvious that the cast are in their element when you watch the episode. Committed to every joke, and more specifically, jokes at their own expense, the core team show that perhaps longevity comes with the ability to poke fun at yourself now and again.

"I don't think I've ever laughed so hard making an episode of a show as

Above: The SG-1 team do *Farscape.*

I did making '200'," smiles Amanda Tapping. "We had so much fun. We sent up everything we've ever wanted to send up. We literally made fun of everything. So that was really fun. We had Carter and O'Neill's wedding, and I always love having Willie Garson on the show – he's just so much fun. I think the *Farscape* send-up was really fun for all of us because Ben and Claudia were there, and the *Star Trek* one was really great.

"It was a big deal. It felt like a really big deal. Two hundred episodes is huge! Not many shows get to that and I was blown away. At first when we started filming it, we were like, 'It's just another episode,' but there was so much energy put into that show and all the writers had a hand in it – it felt special and it felt huge. It felt really big in scope and we all had so much fun on it."

This clear gusto is echoed by Christopher Judge – a man who is covered from head to toe in silver paint to play Tin Man, dons a beard for *Farscape's* D'Argo and looks like Shaft in *Teal'c P.I.*

"I don't think I've ever had more fun being on set," says Judge. "I don't think I've ever had more fun on any episode and getting to play all these different characters. Every department went way above and beyond the call of duty to get those costumes and props and sets done in time and it was all done with laughter and everyone was smiling, everyone was in a great mood. It was just so wonderful that everyone got caught up in the spirit of it and literally took the time to rejoice in what we have accomplished. When you are very close to something, what you have achieved or are achieving is lost on you, because you can't step back and really savor the moment. I was so happy that everyone had the opportunity to do that. That's the most fun I've had shooting anything."

Whilst you don't have to be a follower of *Stargate SG-1* to appreciate the episode in its entirety, it certainly helps. The show pulls off the in-jokes – some more subtle than others – so well, and countless digs are made at the good-humored actors and actresses.

In the *Farscape* sketch, Ben Browder was originally cast to play John Crichton – the role he is known for in science fiction circles across the globe. But he and Shanks switched roles at the last minute, as a nod to the fans who suggested when Browder joined *Stargate* that the two look alike.

Above: Stargate SG-1: *The Teenage Years.*

"The two hundredth episode was a treat," says Shanks. "We got to take the piss out of ourselves left, right and centre. We certainly did it in the one hundredth, and one of the funniest things was that Rob had taken the brunt of. He said to us, 'You guys were upset about the one hundredth episode,' because I was very vocal about it as we weren't really in it a lot, it was mostly about this sort of fictional team. So Rob said, 'Be careful what you wish for!' So all of a sudden we're playing all of these alternate characters and it was a lot of fun for all of us. We joke around here all the time about the show that we're making and the show we really want to be making. This was our chance to actually do that, to live the absurdities of what actually plays in our heads when we're going through certain storylines. We got to play

In Depth: 200

Above: Richard Dean Anderson makes an 'appearance'.

dress-up a little bit, we got to mock a few shows and everyone was a good sport. We were tickled pink to watch the end result, for sure."

But it wasn't only the actors who got to share in the fun onscreen. In a nod to the Jack-Sam fanbase, '200' also features a fantasy wedding of O'Neill and Carter, and if you look closely, you may notice that a lot of the crew were in the wedding scene.

And that's not all. Executive producer Brad Wright makes a cameo appearance as Scotty.

"The *Star Trek* sequence is funny," laughs Wright. "I ended up playing a small part in it which came about as a result of a mix-up. We originally wanted Paul McGillion [*Stargate: Atlantis'* Samuel Beckett] to do it, but last minute there was a mix-up between his agent and us, so I ended up trying on the wardrobe and doing it – it was very funny. I'm glad I did. I used to be an actor, so it was fun for me to step in and do a bad imitation of Scotty. It didn't have to be good – that was the good part! It's not indicative of the series. It's out there, it's something that we could never do if we were on a mainstream network."

Reaching such a milestone as this is an undeniably amazing achievement. Love it or hate it, '200' is a radical departure from *Stargate SG-1's* normal formula. It's unlike any episode they've ever produced, and

everyone who had a hand in making it will certainly remember the laughs that ensued.

Above: *Carter gets ready to say, "I do."*

"It's not like I was going, 'Gee, two hundred!'" shares Wright, candidly. "There's really not any difference. It's like a milestone in age – the difference between turning forty-nine or fifty… It's how it makes you reflect on your life and the experience that it's been. Had it only been nine years, it still would have been a big deal and a lot of fun, and had it gone to eleven? Well, that would have been amazing.

"It's one of those opportunities that you don't get very often though. Some fans loved it, some didn't like it, but we had a helluva good time making it!" Å

Dr Daniel Jackson

Daniel Jackson isn't the man he once was. As the tenth season of *Stargate SG-1* goes on, it's increasingly clear that the archaeological expert has become less awkward and more assertive which each episode. That change is perhaps most acutely reflected by his distinctly physical connection with a certain feisty female alien, as the man behind the false glasses explains...

"I really enjoyed the fact that Claudia Black came in as a regular character," Shanks reveals. "That was the biggest difference between this season and past seasons. We had so much fun on the first six episodes of season nine with Vala, and of course the last episode, 'Crusade'. I really enjoyed having that camaraderie and it was great to have her back for the whole year."

The Daniel-Vala dynamic added the "are they/aren't they?" x-factor that *Stargate SG-1* viewers hadn't seen since O'Neill and Carter. Providing the straight man to what Shanks refers to as Claudia's "infinite clown", Shanks cites their love-hate relationship as his personal highlight of season ten.

"I really enjoyed how they played with it," he smiles. "It's one of those weird things where there is a sort of 'love-interest' but they're also antagonistic towards each other, so it was a nice push-pull with some demonstration of true feelings, yet not breaking the bounds. It's good to keep that friction alive a little bit. And having Claudia aboard was just as much for everybody's daily sanity as it was fun for the show – a nice little spark plug to wander in and get things done."

But what of Daniel himself? The only original character from the *Stargate* movie to be in the television incarnation a decade after the series began, his character has perhaps seen the greatest personal growth of all.

"People always ask me, 'How has your character developed?' and I just say, 'Well, look at how Daniel approaches situations now, and that natural progression of how we've evolved the character,'" shares the actor. "He responds differently in season ten than he would have in season two to certain situations, and that is an expression of his evolution and his growth. You can call it cynicism or baggage or weight, or whatever you want, but he approaches things differently and we wanted to make the character a bit more pragmatic and a bit more hands-on. I really enjoyed the character's less idealistic approach to things and we made him confront certain people and certain situations more than he would have in the past. I really enjoyed that because it seems right for the time spent in the character's soul."

Season ten was not only special for Shanks, but it was a very special season indeed for Daniel. Realizing a life-long dream, Daniel got to take a little trip to the (relatively) lost city of Atlantis in Brad Wright's crossover episode, 'The Pegasus Project'.

"That was a real treat!" Shanks enthuses, clearly thrilled for his character. "Not only to shoot on the *Stargate: Atlantis* sets and hang around with the cast a little, but to have that culmination for Daniel come about where he finally got to go to Atlantis. It was very important to do justice to his ongoing storyline with the Ancients and it was nice to talk about what life was like when he ascended. I think it just delved further into the Ancient storyline and tied it directly into finding some sort of way to diffuse this seemingly unbeatable foe that we created with the Ori. We had to find a weapon to do that, and it was nice to carry on with that storyline.

"I had just mentioned to Brad [Wright] off-hand, 'So, when is Daniel going to go over to Atlantis?' And he said, 'You wanna go?' And I was like, 'The guy spent seven years looking for this place!' That was great for me to do. It's a memorable episode for sure."

As memorable as 'The Pegasus Project' was, the episode that sticks out most in Shanks' mind is the 'Daniel-gone-bad' story, 'The Shroud'. Wanting some time off in the summer to spend with his newborn son, Shanks was written out of a number of episodes in season ten. So what did the show's writers decide to do? Make him a Prior, of course...

"I'll remember that one vividly because I was in make-up for five hours every morning for all seven days of the shoot," winces Shanks. "Of course Rick [Dean Anderson] came back for that and we had a lot of fun doing our routine... but the make-up is what I'll remember the most. I remember reading the script, and my first reaction to it was, 'Let me get this straight: you want to put me in this prosthetic make-up which limits your facial expressions, you want me to put in contacts that kind of blind you and then you want to strap me to a chair and make me talk for thirty-six out of fifty pages? Just talk and tell stories? Wow, this is a tough job for an entertainer

to make interesting!' The problem was that it wasn't just getting into the make-up every day – there was a changeover where I had to be in my normal make-up too. For the first couple of days it was okay, but the stuff that they use to take off the make-up gets in your skin and gives you a rash, and I remember feeling it on the seventh day. If you look at the final scenes of that episode in the infirmary and on the bridge of the *Odyssey*, you can see my skin is just screaming. Under the make-up, my skin

is going, 'Heeelp me!' So I'll remember that for the experience."

Becoming a Prior was only one of a number of dramatic ordeals that Daniel went through in year ten. Almost being killed by Adria, sharing his mind with Merlin and falling in and out of love with Vala are a few more to add to the list.

In the early seasons, Shanks admits to copying James Spader's original portrayal of Daniel Jackson in the *Stargate* movie. But over the years, Shanks has tailored the character to be more like himself. Whilst he claims to be more action-orientated than the intellectual and emotional Jackson, Shanks admits that the gap between the actor and the archaeologist has certainly closed. And this makes it all the more difficult to say goodbye.

"When we were shooting our last episode, we didn't yet know that the movies were going to be happening – so everybody was kind of emotional," offers Shanks. "It was the end of something big. Ten years of our lives were coming to a close. If we'd walked out of the stage and they'd started dismantling it, we would have run back in and saved the furniture.

"I don't think there's a way, a completely satisfactory way to tie up the show to please me or anybody else. Just make sure that we live on in the imagination of the audience, and in my imagination too, of having those characters go off into the universe, with smiles on their faces." Å

Lieutenant Colonel Cameron Mitchell

Over the years, actor Ben Browder has developed quite a resume of television appearances: *Melrose Place*, *Murder, She Wrote* and *CSI: Miami* are just a few which grace the long list, highlights of which include a recurring spot in *Party of Five*, and most memorably, as John Crichton in *Farscape*. But his most recent work as Lieutenant Colonel Cameron Mitchell on *Stargate SG-1* has not only given Browder an unexpected further-increasing fan base, it's given him two years of "fun, laughter and life-long friends."

Having been brought in to lead Stargate Command's flagship team last year, Browder has now shed his 'new guy' moniker. And just as Mitchell has become more comfortable in his role within SG-1, so too has the ever smiling actor behind him.

"I liked the way Mitchell developed in season ten, I like the way he's settled in throughout the year," shares Browder. "Season ten was more comfortable. Every set has its own culture, it has its own pace and rhythm and in the first year my job was to learn that. So I took a bit of time in season nine finding a way to fit in, and season ten kind of went by like the junior year of high school – you're there, you know the ropes, you know who you're having lunch with and it's good that way."

Whilst Mitchell's unfailing enthusiasm brought a new energy to the show and the SG-1 team, Browder's fellow cast members and crew sing the same song about the animated actor. In a typically self-deprecating fashion, the talented actor and writer (though he will most certainly deny this title), is hesitant of taking any kind of credit for the success of *Stargate SG-1*, and only manages to focus the praise elsewhere.

"Our cast is just great," says Browder. "It's a very comfortable cast to be around and it's filled with very intelligent people. You look around and you realise that they're all really bright. Chris [Judge], Mike [Shanks], Amanda [Tapping], Claudia [Black], and Beau [Bridges], they're all just very bright, articulate, interesting, funny people, so coming to work is a joy. We have a cast that gets on terribly well – we laugh all the time, we have a lot of fun and there really are no problems. It's a great place to work, and there are times when you have more fun than should be allowed, and be paid for."

It's clear that just like the more veteran actors of the show, Browder has enjoyed his time as Cameron Mitchell all the more for his on-set experiences off-camera, but he also admits to having a soft spot for his counterpart.

"I liked who Mitchell was," shares Browder matter-of-factly. "I think that by the time we finished, Mitchell was well integrated into the show. Obviously there are a lot of things that you could address, but the show has run for ten years. Every character has a lot of baggage and Mitchell

doesn't have as much baggage because he was only there for two years, and *Stargate SG-1* is not a purely character-driven show. There are a lot of plot-driven episodes, and the series itself is driven by the device known as the Stargate, so in a certain sense, the characters service those plots and service those stories. If you had ten years you would learn more about Mitchell, but I think for two years we know enough. It's that thing where you can know someone for ten years and they'll do something and you'll say, 'Wow, I didn't know that about you,' and that's true of life as well – the idea of a character as a rigid construct isn't particularly interesting or effective storytelling. But Mitchell still has lots of secrets…"

And what sort of secrets might they be?

"Well, where does he go on Friday nights?" Browder deadpans. "He says he's going to watch movies, but that may not be the case… Why does he only eat peanut butter and jelly sandwiches? And where are the bathrooms at the SGC? Fairly important questions by anyone's standards."

Jokes aside, season ten certainly answered some questions about Mitchell. Ever since he stepped foot into the SGC, he's had to cope with one dilemma after the other. This year, he's had to infiltrate the Lucian Alliance, come face to face with bounty hunters at his high school reunion, and save the planet a couple of times for good measure. But Mitchell is a guy who has been able to sustain a sense of calmness. And it seems that life imitates art, as Browder, too, takes everything in his stride.

This season, a particularly memorable episode for the actor was 'Uninvited', when Mitchell and Landry retreat to O'Neill's secluded cabin for some well-earned rest-and-relaxation.

"We don't call that 'Uninvited', we call that 'Brokeback Stargate'," smiles Browder. "Landry and Mitchell in the mountains? It made sense because *Brokeback Mountain* had come out at that time, and the writers said, 'We're going to explore the relationship between Mitchell and Landry and they're going to be in a cabin up in the hills.' I went, 'Just don't do 'Brokeback Stargate', that's all I ask! I think that's pushing it, even for me!' – 'Here General Landry, let me show you how to handle a gun... Allow me to reload that weapon for you, sir...'"

Despite the important role of his character in season ten, Browder believes that there aren't any Mitchell-centric episodes this season. However, he plays a large part in 'Univited', 'Company of Thieves', 'Road Not Taken' and 'Bounty' in particular, taking on the subtly essential role of the everyman – someone for the show's viewers to relate to.

"You know what, it was fine," explains Browder of his character's involvement this year. "To a certain degree, it was enjoyable to take a back-seat. That's not to say that as an actor you don't want to go, 'Ah, here is my hammer!' but that wasn't part of season ten. And that was fine with me. The Ori storyline is heavily centered on Vala and Daniel, and that's a major chunk of the story right there. So Mitchell's through-line is a much quieter through-line, which is more about facilitating the other team members and their story arcs, and Mitchell's sort of carrying the story arc going, 'Hello, how do we do this? How are we going to solve that?'"

Had the series continued, it's clear that Mitchell could have provided a rich source for story material. But, now that the show is finished, how does Browder think his future career in television and film is likely to progress? The actor gives the seasoned grin of someone well attuned to a business where you are forever starting over.

"The great thing is that I love doing what I do already and I find that it's not that hard to come across things that you love doing," he answers, in a typically upbeat manner. "Life has so many fascinating things to do. Hopefully, if I'm lucky, I'll get another acting job. I've been very lucky that my life has been good, but I've always sort of had that happy disposition. It's hard for me to stay grumpy for very long, and you look around and you think of all the possibilities. It's an amazing world and there's all these things to be done, but at the end of the day, I've still got to make my crust. We've graduated *Stargate SG-1* – I guess we have to go out and grow up now..." Å

Lieutenant Colonel Samantha Carter

Since she first exchanged sardonic quips with O'Neill at the SGC, Samantha Carter has emerged as one of the most beloved characters on *Stargate SG-1*, in no small part due to the sense of humor, intelligence, and humility of actress Amanda Tapping.

It's been eleven years since Tapping first auditioned for the part of Captain Samantha Carter. Since then, her character has had to cope with the death of countless loved ones, alien attacks, slavery, torture and constant enemy threats of world domination. Having breathed life into SG-1's science expert and theoretical astrophysicist for over a decade, it comes as no surprise to hear that she's grown attached to her alter ego.

"I like Sam," smiles the actress. "I think there's been a really nice evolution for her over the ten seasons and now that she has moved over to *Stargate: Atlantis* there's a whole new side to her. Aside from season ten, to be honest, I feel like there has been a challenge every year and that there was an evolution for the character. As much as I've come into my own as a woman, Sam Carter's come into her own as a woman. There's a maturity to her now and a depth that gives her more soul and it's through the relationships she's had and it's through the experiences she's had that she's really come into her own... I like her. She's a nice gal. I feel like in a lot of ways, my growing up has been channeled into Sam. There's definitely a symbiotic relationship now, the lines are so blurry between the two of us, whereas it was delineated before. But it was bound to happen after ten years."

When she is playing Samantha Carter, Tapping gives it everything she's got. Like her counterpart, she is both dedicated and determined, and it's a rare thing to see Tapping not laughing or smiling on set. But unlike Sam, Tapping is a triple-role woman – wife, mother and actress. When she is at home being a mother to her young daughter, Olivia, Tapping gives it her heart and soul.

"The hardest element of my life is being a working mum and finding the balance there. I think I've found a pretty good balance though. Olivia is a really happy, well-adjusted, secure little girl with a great little sense of humor, so hopefully I've succeeded at least thus far. I love my career, but being a mum is far more important."

The big career news, her role in *Stargate SG-1*'s sister show *Stargate: Atlantis*, is, of course, cause for celebration, but it has not gone to Tapping's head. With no false modesty, she brushes congratulations aside by deflecting the compliments elsewhere.

"I'm really grateful," she gushes. "It's an embarrassment of riches for me now to go to *Stargate: Atlantis*. I'm having a blast! How great is this – I get

Lieutenant Colonel Samantha Carter

to stay in the city that I love and raise my daughter here. To have constant work is such a rarity, and it feels like a whole new show and it feels like a whole new character in some ways for me, so it's interesting. People are like, 'Oh my god, another year playing Carter?' but it's a whole new Carter, and I don't look at it as, 'Oh, it's my eleventh year playing the same character!' It doesn't feel like I've been playing the same character for ten years at all. I certainly hope that the audience hasn't got bored of me yet! The producers, god bless them, have been really great, Sci Fi has been great, MGM has been great. I'm a very lucky girl," she smiles.

Ten seasons and 215 episodes have ensured that *Stargate SG-1* has a place in television history, but for the woman behind Carter, it's not the professional accomplishment that matters, but the personal one.

"What will I take from my experience of this show?" ponders Tapping. "Just the sense of family and the sense of community and being a part of something special. That's a gift in this industry to have that. Not only the longevity but also the sense of family that we've always had. That sense of joy about what we do. At the end of the day we're all still laughing. Every day we're laughing our asses off and having a great time. And that's what I'll take away from this experience – how much fun I've had over the past ten years with these wonderful people. What a gift to play this character and be a part of a monumental show and to have it last as long as it has and to have made the friends I have made – it's been amazing."

Before MGM had greenlit the movies, Tapping was faced with the heart-wrenching process of saying goodbye to the show that had become such a huge part of her life. The last episode, 'Unending', was a particularly memorable moment from season ten.

"'Unending' was really a hard episode to do – we laughed a lot and we cried a lot. The beauty of it was the very last shot on the very last day was set up so that we would walk through the Stargate, and that was awesome. It felt like we had come full circle. After the tears on the last day, Christopher, Michael and I snuck away at the end of it all and went to look down at the Stargate. We had been on this set together since 1997 and we saw the Stargate together for the first time. I remember when we first saw it, we were like, 'Oh my god, we're on this huge show!' and of course we had come full circle at the end and we stood looking down at the Stargate and said, 'Wow...'"

Now that she's able to reflect on her time on *Stargate SG-1*, what does Tapping believe to be the secret of the show's success?

"We all find joy in what we're doing, and I think that translates onto the screen – the joy of what we do," says the actress. "We all feel this way, and that's perhaps part of the formula that has allowed the success of the show. I know people who have worked in offices for ten years and they're miserable and hate getting up to go to work every day. I don't hate getting up – well, some mornings I do, of course – but by the time I'm in my car and driving to work, I'm in a great mood.

"I know I sound like Suzy freakin' Sunshine and Pollyanna, but you know what? Pollyanna works for me. There are really no ripples on this lake – I'm pretty happy. The sun rises and the sun sets and I'm doing exactly what I want to do between those hours." Å

Teal'c

espite portraying a man of few words, Chris Judge has made an indelible mark on *Stargate SG-1*, breathing life into reserved Jaffa Teal'c for ten seasons. "Season ten felt like the last *Rocky* movie for me," says the actor with an infectious chuckle which immediately separates him from his more serious counterpart. "This year felt like two seasons, actually. I think that we expected the show to go for another season, so once we found out that it was cancelled, the second half of the season really became about celebrating each other and really taking the time to enjoy and reflect over the last ten years. We made sure not to take the experience for granted as we knew it was going to end."

An inveterate raconteur, Judge is more removed from his character on . *Stargate SG-1* than perhaps any other cast-member. Whilst Teal'c is stoic, Judge is playful. Teal'c thinks there is a definite time and place for jokes, whereas Judge thinks there's always time for a joke – occasionally to the frustration of his bosses.

"I certainly enjoyed playing Teal'c, but it was tough," offers the actor. "One of the hardest things about playing Teal'c is his absolute dryness. Things that I found hysterical, I had to play very straight. To the Jaffa, Teal'c's a very funny guy – he's like a comedian to them, so I always tried to play that aspect underneath his exterior. He's definitely got funnier as the seasons have gone on, and to have that realized was great fun for me.

"Actually, in season nine Robert Cooper called me into his office. I had overtly tried to have Teal'c smile more and Coop was like, 'We love what you're doing with Teal'c, but it might be just a bit too much, so maybe just take it down a few notches.' He showed me a few examples and I was like, 'Yeah… Maybe you're right!' They've always been very good about having a two-way dialogue. In a lot of shows it's just, 'Shut up, actors – just say the words.' If there's anything that bothers you here, or you wonder why your character does certain things, there's an open-door policy. It's a very supportive and nurturing environment."

With a name that means 'strength' in the Jaffa language, Teal'c has consistently displayed exactly that. A proud warrior, he usually exhibits a calm attitude and great self-restraint. However, in one episode this season, we are allowed a glimpse of a more passionate and enraged part of his character.

"'Talion' was the last episode where I had the A-story and that I featured heavily in," says Judge. "I thought it was really a great episode – not only for closure for Teal'c, but also closure for me as an actor playing Teal'c. It really came full circle as it went back to Teal'c being a warrior and the character he was in the earlier seasons. The fact that it was directed by Andy Mikita, who was the first AD [assistant director] on the pilot, I thought was really a

fitting end for both me and Teal'c.

"It's been a few years since there's been a real kickass Teal'c episode. This definitely gets back to that. It was the fiercest, bloodiest *Stargate SG-1* we've ever done by a long way. We had to cut back on it quite a bit in editing! It was very satisfying work because we worked hard and we enjoyed it. There was a lot of training. I had to rehearse the fight scenes whilst we were shooting 'Family Ties'. When I was rehearsing a fight, one of the stuntmen hit me on the forehead so it opened up a gash and I had nine stitches. So in 'Family Ties' you see a lot of scenes with Teal'c thinking with his hand to his head – that's to cover up my stitches!"

'Family Ties' is a memorable episode for Judge, and for his fans, as it showcases what a source of humor Teal'c's stoic nature can be. His final scene at the theater – watching a show similar to the *Vagina Monologues* – provides the comic relief that *Stargate SG-1* is so clearly adored for. This movement away from the fundamental 'Teal'c' is something that Judge notes was more prevalent in the previous seasons, and whilst he so obviously delights in dramatizing a more relaxed, amusing side to his alter ego, he equally enjoys taking Teal'c back to his combatant roots.

"In seasons seven, eight and nine, Teal'c had really become more of an orator – he was talking a lot more and had these huge monologues. He really got away from being the warrior, the guy he was at the beginning. I think that in season ten, the writers made a concerted effort to get him back to where he first was. To run that gamut, to have gone and come back to where he started,

with obviously a lot more knowledge and a lot more insight into where and who he is, I thought was perfect. I've just been so fortunate that we've had ten years to bring Teal'c's progression along naturally – it's been a real blessing."

Spending a decade on a show that he loves, surrounded by people who have become his best friends, is what Judge counts as his biggest blessing of all.

"No matter what was going on, we were always able to laugh," he explains. "I think that we are, or we were, an anomaly in this business because there was very little hierarchy between cast, crew and producers. We still to this day go away and socialize together. We go on golfing trips – me, the producers, the crew – so to have that personally is something so incredible that, unfortunately, I don't think I will ever experience in this business again. Actors [usually] love to commiserate about working – show me a working actor and I'll show you an unhappy actor.

"As much as I'll miss working with these guys," Judge adds, typically looking on the bright side, "I'll be able to be around my kids more and I'll get to go to all their plays and all their sporting events and just hang around and *be* with them – go to the park and just be a dad."

So will he miss Teal'c?

"Yeah, of course," he answers decisively, "but I'll miss the people far more. For ten years I got up in the morning and I was happy about going to work. I'm going to miss that. Who would ever have thought ten years ago that we'd still be around now, still be doing good stuff, still be as popular as ever and still be laughing?" ᛉ

When General Jack O'Neill was promoted to oversee Homeworld Security, he carefully handpicked his mentor to be his successor. Stepping out of retirement to replace him was O'Neill's long-time friend, General Hank Landry, and replacing fan-favorite Richard Dean Anderson was prolific actor Beau Bridges.

"Landry is an interesting man," begins Bridges. "Landry's a leader, but he's got a sense of humor. He can be tough when he needs to be, but he's got problems at home and that makes him more human. I think that's what we tend to forget about leaders and presidents and generals and people in power: even though they have this huge calling, which is their job, they're people just like the rest of us, with all the human concerns that we have."

Taking on the daunting task of commanding the SGC for the final two seasons of *Stargate SG-1*, Bridges admits to being slightly nervous when he first took on the role of Landry, so going into his second year, there was one big difference for both the actor and his character.

"Season ten was my second season with the show and I was really much more relaxed as an actor in the group. By that time I'd had a whole season with the rest of the troops and felt really comfortable – and I think General Landry did as well. He was less of a hardass and he started to have a little bit more fun... as did I. He's a great leader."

Being a leader is an important part of both Landry's life and Bridges'. The actor lists two men who impressed and inspired him in his early life: his actor father, Lloyd Bridges, and his college basketball coach, John Wooden, who Bridges describes as "one of the most successful college basketball coaches that ever lived."

"My father was a leader in many respects when he was working," says Bridges. "He always led by example, and never shouted at people. I like that. His favorite word was 'respect'. Demand that, starting of course with yourself. You've got to respect yourself, respect all the members of the team, and if you're the leader, you demand that they respect each other, too.

"John Wooden was also a great man. He won ten straight national championships and he was also a man of few words. He used to say, 'Make every day your masterpiece,' so he was coming from a very positive side – but he didn't take any crap from anybody. These are the men that helped me to come up with General Landry."

When Bridges was approached to play Landry, the character was a blank page. Robert Cooper invited him to work on the character's backstory and flesh him out, so Bridges understandably feels a close connection to the character that he had a hand in creating. With *Stargate SG-1* going into its ninth successful year before Bridges joined the close cast, did he find it

General Hank Landry

challenging to join the established show?

"Not challenging," he muses. "I just felt lucky to be part of something like this. I have had a really good time with General Landry. I really felt a responsibility towards the fans because they've been so genuine and they're there for the show consistently, and that's why I'm so happy also that they did these two two-hour movies. They really owe it to the fans to bring some closure. Maybe we'll do some more, who knows?"

A self-confessed fan of science fiction, Bridges' career boasts an impressive list of film and television roles such as *The Fabulous Baker Boys*, *Jerry Maguire*, and more recently, *The Good German* with George Clooney. Perhaps he, more than anyone, is in a position to decipher what traits have allowed *Stargate SG-1* to continue for so many years.

"I think the stories themselves," he answers. "I think 'the play's the thing', as Shakespeare said. Brad Wright and Robert Cooper are certainly two of the best execs in the business – they write great stories. I also think that in the genre of science fiction, *Stargate SG-1* is one of the first ones that came in with a tremendous sense of humor, which is absent from a lot of sci-fi. A lot of sci-fi shows take themselves very seriously and *Stargate SG-1* never has, which I think is probably mostly due to Richard Dean Anderson's contribution in the beginning – that kind of off-center, weird sense of humor gives the show a certain and unique style."

This season, along with Bridges' new-found comfort playing Landry, came a display of the general's own unique sense of humor – in no way comparable to that of O'Neill, but equally amusing. Perhaps the most memorable episode for Landry this season is 'Uninvited', where he takes a rather apathetic Mitchell to a country retreat for a weekend of male bonding.

"I loved 'Uninvited' this season," laughs Bridges, "especially when it suddenly turned out that the general was interested in birds – that caught my eye when I read the script, because I love birds! When I was teasing my youngest, who's now fifteen – he's not that young anymore – but when he was a little guy, we had a bird call we did. The two of us would do bird calls and then, as he got older, I started to embarrass him. I'd say purposefully in front of his friends, 'I think it's time for a bird cry.' And he'd say, 'Dad!' So I had the same kind of thing going with Mitchell in the cabin with the birds.

"When I did the bird call I was just fooling around and it came out of nowhere. I don't know where it came from," he laughs, taking great pleasure in demonstrating his very impressive bird call.

Bridges has a long list of upcoming roles – he's bagged a part in the award-winning television comedy *My Name is Earl*, and he's recently worked with Sarah Jessica Parker and Mischa Barton. But the softly-spoken actor speaks very fondly of his time, albeit not very long in comparison to some of the others, on the show.

"I think that it's always fun to have some longevity in the role," he explains. "Over a period of two years there's forty episodes and it's great to get to track a guy all through those experiences. It's more like life, so that has been fun. I've done that a couple of times in my career, but not often, so it's been great. I really like this cast and the crew, so it's been a very positive experience." Å

Vala Mal Doran

From the moment a leather-clad Claudia Black appeared in Stargate Command it was clear that we would be seeing a lot more of lovable con-artist Vala Mal Doran. The feisty alien not only gained the trust, respect and approval of the ever-cautious members of SG-1, but, more importantly, of the show's passionate fan base. Proving just as popular, actress Claudia Black found her own place in the close-knit group that is *Stargate SG-1*, winning the hearts of cast and crew alike and earning a regular spot in season ten.

"Vala is great fun," Claudia Black says, smiling. "It's been such a privilege to play her. And considering that she wasn't a character that was expected, necessarily, to be continued, I've had a little bit of a hand in how she grew. I've almost been an influence from day one, because it was anybody's guess as to where she was going to go, and what she was going to do. She's such a fun, brilliant character to play."

Instrumental in kick-starting season ten, Vala was not only the newest member of the show, she was its focal point. Driving the burgeoning Ori storyline forward, the season opened with Vala trapped in the Ori galaxy, having given birth to Adria, the Orici. From the outset, it was clear that the common farcical Vala moments the audience had grown to expect were going to give way to something far more serious and dramatic.

"It's an interesting turn this season as we see a lot more of Vala's backstory revealed," explains Black. "It's been fantastic. Vala's an amazing character to play. She's very different to the last character I played and that's always a real incentive to accept a role, to extend yourself and do something different, to take risks. Robert Cooper's been very supportive of that. Vala's just been a really great foil for everybody. During the last seasons of a long-running show you do need to bring in someone or something to mix things up a bit and I think she was the perfect candidate. She, of course, had a child this season and got married, so she's changed from being a single renegade who always flies solo – she's now got quite the entourage from when she started."

Surrounding herself with people she cares about, and more importantly, people who care about her, is a new experience for Vala. Throughout the season, her relationships with each member of SG-1 grow and mature in their own distinct way. Most absorbing to watch, however, is her friendship with Daniel Jackson. And just as Vala's unlikely friendship with the archaeologist has blossomed, so the actors' friendship has also.

"The highlights for me this season are always any opportunity I have to do the Daniel and Vala scenes," says Black, who struck up an instant rapport with Shanks. "I really love working with Michael, we have a great laugh together. I haven't seen him that much this season on set, we haven't done as much stuff together, but just all the laughing we've had everyday is so great.

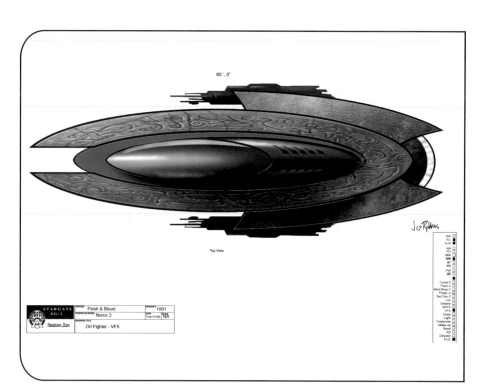

60', 0"

Top View

J.c.D.Robbins

STARGATE SG-1	EPISODE Flesh & Blood	EPISODE # 1001
	SCENE/LOCATION Norco 3	DATE Feb 01/06	SCALE NA
Season Ten	DRAWING TITLE Ori Fighter - VFX		

"Fluffy"

sC 34

A Dragon rises up out of the dark pit....

Fireball blocked by shield

TILT UP DRAGON MOVES CLOSER

and hovers over them.

Over Mitchell. The Dragon turns and...

Mitchell

lashes out with it's tail
Note. Plate shot -remove "broken" stalagmites

The Dragon throws it's head back and...

Sc 37

VFX cave exit on location

loosens a fireball right at them.

Sc 38

POV of volcano as the Dragon bursts out

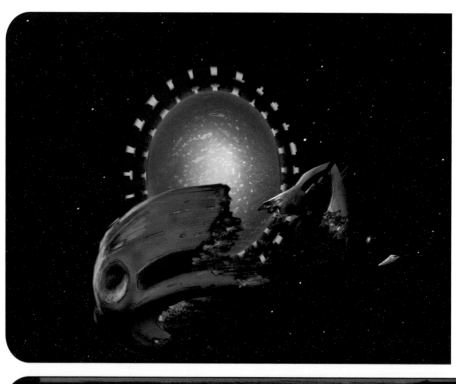

Construction - flat wall as exterior cargo ship - install on location at angle

greens provide mound
of dirt along flat wall

Greens - place ferns as per illustration

Construction/Set Dec - add one

Furling City - Concept

No matter how bad the hours are, we still find a way to giggle our way through it."

As entertaining as she is irritating, the character of Vala is an enigma of sorts. But season ten certainly gave more depth to the character and helped the audience understand that her tough and blunt exterior is little more than a façade. It is Daniel, more so than anyone else, who sees the true Vala. Instrumental in convincing General Landry to let Vala join SG-1, Daniel consistently fights her corner.

"I think Vala's friendship with Daniel is a genuine friendship now, and I think it's really sweet to see the show go that way, because they really obviously do care for each other," shares Black. "He's been a huge influence on her ability to open up and be vulnerable and clear some past issues that she hadn't had the time to, because she's been too busy trying to survive and being on the run."

A strong female character, Vala is made more human by her fallible nature. Is there a thin line between where Claudia ends and Vala begins?

"Oh, there has to be, there has to be," answers Black assertively. "I'm her in corporeal form and whatever is coming out of my mouth, there's got to

be stuff from me. And I think it's hard for people that know me well to watch my performances because they'll say, 'Vala laughs the way that you do,' and I say, 'Well, don't be daft, of course she does!' If I'm going to be natural in the moment, I'm not going to concoct a laugh unless I'm playing a very masked character. Though certain aspects of my performance in any character I play are going to be influenced by other people as well as myself, and contextually you hope that you give the impression that you're playing someone else. Really my job is to just convince people who are watching that it's possible that I could be that person."

In the relatively short time that she's been part of *Stargate SG-1*, Black has certainly convinced the audience to believe in, and care for, the character of Vala Mal Doran. Before Vala, science fiction fans knew Black for her portrayal of *Farscape*'s Aeryn Sun. The show ran for four years, culminating in a mini-series, so Black is no stranger to working on a successful television series. With *Stargate SG-1* lasting an amazing ten years, the actress attributes the show's record breaking performance to the all-important "chemistry" between the actors – amongst other things.

"It's fundamental to the show's success," explains Black. "I think that in science fiction, you have, if you are lucky, a very loyal and intelligent audience. It was an established brand, the Stargate itself is iconic, and it was a very interesting concept for a feature film, and it's an indication of the world. You turn on the TV and you're always going to find *Stargate SG-1*, and in a way that's what makes the show's departure not so bitter – the sweetness is that you're always going to be able to find it, like *Seinfeld* or *Star Trek*. I think the writing has much to do with the show's success – they never took themselves too seriously. I think that's important, especially in sci-fi, because that way you're never above the medium and you don't take yourself too seriously."

We know little about Vala's early life – it's perhaps the biggest loss of the show's cancellation that we won't get the chance to find out more about this interesting woman who disguises her true, sensitive nature with humor and awkward jokes. The fans of *Stargate SG-1* will no doubt miss the character of Vala, and Black herself will miss her new friends terribly.

"The people are the crème de la crème for me on this show in particular," smiles Black. "The overriding thing for me has pretty much just been the laughter – it's terrific. Sometimes it could have helped to take things a little more seriously, but I wouldn't trade the laughter for anything. It's been the most wonderful lesson and very, very cool people work on this show and the cast is exceptional. How they get on and how welcoming they were, where I was concerned, was just amazing. I love my new buddies and I'm not prepared to say goodbye." Å

Recurring Characters

"After all that time we spent together, you still know nothing about me."

Season ten of *Stargate SG-1* saw the return of many familiar characters in guest roles. The most notable of these was **Richard Dean Anderson**. Having taken a break from *Stargate SG-1*, it was surely only fitting that Anderson reprise his role as Jack O'Neill – now a General, no less – for the final season. Though the character would be continuing to appear as a guest star in spin-off show *Stargate: Atlantis* for fans of the original show, having him rejoin the team in anniversary episode '200' was a wonderful way to round off ten years of *Stargate SG-1* adventures. The part also displayed Anderson's trademark wit,

including a scene in which he appears as an 'invisible' version of himself. According to executive producer Brad Wright, the scene was written in so that they could incorporate the character into the two hundredth episode. At the time the production had thought that Anderson himself wouldn't be available, so the 'invisible' gag was a way of including him without having to actually shoot with the actor. In an ironic but somehow entirely fitting twist, however, Anderson ended up playing himself in the scene, donning a bright green head-to-toe suit so that the visual effects department could later erase him from the take. Thankfully, that wasn't the last fans would see of the character – not least since General O'Neill would be returning in the second of *Stargate SG-1*'s movies, *Stargate: Continuum*.

There were some new faces

added to the extensive list of *SG-1* recurring guest stars in season ten. **Morena Baccarin**, for example, who was brought on board to play Vala's Ori daughter, Adria, will be best known to viewers for her role as Inara Serra in Joss Whedon's short-lived but acclaimed series *Firefly*. Born in Rio de Janeiro, Brazil, Baccarin moved to the United States at the age of ten and spent her early years in New York, where she won a place at the Julliard School of Dance, Drama and Music. *Firefly* gave Baccarin her biggest role, and since then she has featured in various other television series, including *The O.C*, *How I Met Your Mother*, and as recurring character Nurse Jessica Kivala in *Heartland*. "I love the character," Baccarin revealed of Adria to thescifiworld.net. "She is truly evil. The worst kinds of people are the ones with no acceptance and she is one of those. What she believes is the word of god. And I get to wear really cool contacts... Though it was pretty comical watching me get around feeling the walls with my contact lenses on!"

One face that viewers had seen before but had not had much time to get to know, was that of **Tim Guinee**. Having appeared at the conclusion of season nine as Vala's devoted but somewhat misguided (and misled) husband, Tomin, Guinee was called back for season ten as the battle against the Ori heated up. Born and bred in Los Angeles, the actor's extensive television credit list includes shows such as all three *CSI* series, *Without A Trace*, *Medium*, and a recurring role in

supernatural drama *Ghost Whisperer* with Jennifer Love Hewitt.

Season ten also featured many faces that viewers have grown to know and love over the years. Returning to *Stargate SG-1* as the Goa'uld-who-just-wouldn't-die, **Cliff Simon** once again reprised his role as Ba'al – or more accurately, as many Ba'als, since SG-1 still had to contend with his multiple clone selves. "He's outdone Anubis," the actor proudly told gateworld.net. "I'm now the longest-running villain on the show, which is pretty amazing. I never thought... five seasons? Wow!"

Born in Johannesburg, South Africa, Simon's first love was swimming, and he aspired to join his country's Olympic team before becoming a model and participating in the 1992 'Mr South Africa' contest, the prize for which included a part in a soap opera. Winning the contest launched Simon's career as an actor, which eventually led to his relocation to Los Angeles and his recurring role in *Stargate SG-1*.

Having been introduced as new Chief Medical Officer Dr Carolyn Lam in season nine, **Lexa Doig** returned to further flesh out her character in season ten. As General Landry's estranged daughter, the character had always been intended as a way to develop Landry's personal life, and season ten gave both Doig and her on-screen father, Beau Bridges, more of a chance to do just that. In 'Family Ties,' for example, Lam worked to get her separated parents into a civilized conversation.

Bill Dow, who returned once more as Dr Bill Lee, will be recognizible to some viewers from one of his previous recurring roles – as Dr 'Chuck' Burke in long-running science fiction series *The X-Files*. As one of the Vancouver acting fraternity, Dow has featured in many different shows shooting in the area, including *The 4400*, *Da Vinci's Inquest*, *Pasadena*, and *Kyle XY*. An accomplished – and award-winning – theater actor, Dow has also directed several acclaimed productions at The Vancouver Playhouse.

Last, but by no means least, **Tony Amendola** reprised his role as Teal'c's mentor and great friend, Bra'tac. Having begun his association with *Stargate SG-1* in the show's very first season, Amendola continued to evolve his character right until the series' conclusion. The veteran actor and star of films such as *The Mask of Zorro* feels that his role on *Stargate SG-1* is one of the most endearing and truthful parts he has played. Working with the regular cast, and with Christopher Judge in particular, was one of the best experiences of his career so far.

"Sometimes you have to work very hard – you have to imagine the person is someone other than they are," Amendola explains. "The actor receives from another actor, and also can endow another actor – the classic thing is, the king doesn't play the king, it's everyone around the king that makes him the king. With Chris, it was very easy. I had no idea [at first] who this person was that was so pivotal. We just looked at each other, at each other's eyes, and smiled. I don't know quite why, but I knew it was going to be great, I knew it was going to be fine. I knew there was a lot to respect. I saw a lot of warmth, I saw a lot of fierceness, a lot of intelligence. His respect for me as a character elevates me as an actor." Å

Costumes

Valerie Halverson

Stargate SG-1's tenth and final year produced a variety of challenges for the show's talented costume department. Though the series had always sported a vast array of different garments derived both from Earth's history and the designers' own ideas, the basis of the show's costume repertoire was most often military. In season ten, several factors meant that the designers found themselves increasingly designing non-military costumes, which allowed the designers to let their imaginations roam. The department began the year under the guidance of Christine Mooney, who had started designing for the show in season nine. Later in the season, this task was assumed by Valerie Halverson.

"In season ten we brought in more people from other worlds, so it was less military," Halverson explains. "Ba'al had been established, but Adria was quite new to us at the end of season nine."

Adria's costumes provided the first challenge of the season, since her rapid growth at the beginning of season ten called for a succession of progressive outfits. "It was a bit overwhelming from a construction point of view, but we loved that idea," laughs the designer. "Christine Mooney was still designing the show at that point and the great thing was she was able to create the same look from a two year-old to a six year-old to a twelve year-old. She did an excellent job on that. And then the next time we saw Adria I was on the show and she was full-grown and the leader of her people. It was really fun to do that, because she was still an adolescent at heart. So the first costume we put her in was a bit of a warrior look, and we did it that way because it was almost as if she went shopping and she thought the Ori warriors looked fantastic so she wanted an outfit just like that – but she was still a bit of a princess in her head, so we made it almost like a teenage version of that. We had a lot of fun with Adria because her character wasn't very mature, but she still liked having new clothes. She was a dream to make stuff for because it wasn't military – it was really fun."

The department was also charged with finding an appropriate way to integrate the most wayward resident of the SGC, Vala, into the SG-1 team. Since Vala first

Below: The SG-1 ladies hit the shops.

appeared in *Stargate SG-1*, her character was clearly more likely to choose clothing designed to raise eyebrows than to fit in with the rest of her colleagues. In season ten, however, Vala was destined to be an integral part of the SG-1 team, and there was no question of Earth's military allowing her to continue wearing whatever she liked as she stepped through the gate. The decision was taken to introduce her to the concept of a uniform, but of course this was Vala, and part of her character is to be individual. It was down to the costume department to find ways to reflect that individuality despite the fact that Vala was now often in battle dress uniforms.

Above: With Vala came some great outfits.

"We certainly took some liberties with her uniform," admits Halverson. "She still liked to have this quirky side. Claudia [Black] liked to bring that out, so I think she had discussions with the writers about that. It made everything a little bit quirky for everyone else as well – her influence on everything made it less military. There's an episode called 'Family Ties' where Vala and Carter go shopping, and it's one of the few times that you see Carter really embracing the civilian look. So I think Vala had a lot to do with that, breaking the rules a bit. Especially in the series finale, where they were all stuck on the ship. She would end up putting brooches on and wearing a different top with the uniform pants. Vala was the most dramatic departure from the uniform of all of them. We did some things like adding jewelry to tank tops and things like that. Basically [the idea was] she was doing crafts in her room because she was bored, whereas the other

Costumes

characters just tended to wear their clothes out."

Costumes are always a reflection and an accentuation of the character wearing them. This being the case, choosing the right form of garment is particularly important when a character puts on something different to what the audience is accustomed to seeing them wear. A perfect example of this is when the SG-1 team members don civilian outfits instead of their more usual military garb, of which there were several instances in season ten.

"You have to be really in tune to the character at that point," Halverson explains of choosing the right type of civilian outfit. "Like, it wasn't much of a departure for Landry because he was a lifer military man, and Mitchell was still fairly conservative. Yet some of the other guys could go a little bit more casual. Teal'c, he always had to cover up because he had his Goa'uld

Above: Ba'al is one of Halverson's favorite characters to outfit.

tattoo on his head, so that would dictate what we would do with him – always having to wear a hat and such. Generally, if our top cast were going into civilian clothes, we really had to consider that character, how military they were or how civilian they were in their character."

In the middle of the season, the crew geared up for the celebratory two hundredth episode, an extravaganza of sets, locations and costumes that would have surely made a lesser department shudder. Not Mooney and Halverson, however, despite the breathtaking amount of costumes that needed to be created.

"That was amazing," Halverson recalls. "Christine Mooney was still designing then, and she did a fantastic, farcical take on things. I think that was probably her most fun one she did. It was a daunting task. I have to say, after that we slept in a corner for a couple of days! We made every single [costume], including the *Farscape* ones. We even made the mask that Ben [Browder] ended up wearing. We cast that in our model shop."

One of the most-awaited costumes they designed was for the Furlings, a race of creatures that had been spoken of since the very first season of *Stargate SG-1* but never actually seen. Halverson reports that the initial design ideas for these little furry critters came from executive producers Brad Wright and Robert Cooper.

"They really had a feeling, a pre-conceived notion," she explains. "They wanted them to be friendly and welcoming, and I think that they really were! They were so fantastic. We have some obscure sources over

Above: The Furling actors try not to lose their heads.

here that we've found through [the] years, and we just happened to see that [fur fabric] and thought that it was a little bit non-Earth-like. The Furlings were living in the trees as well and it had a bit of a camouflage feel to it. It was a bit of a challenge to design something that went over not only a small person but then also a prosthetic and a suit. So it wasn't really a person shape we had worked with before. That was a challenge, but I think that the fabrications all worked with it. It was a very collaborative effort with the model shop. It was fun to do.

"Ba'al has always been one of my favorites," concludes the designer, regarding which characters she most likes to produce costumes for. "He's such a great character. And [Cliff Simon] is such a great guy to costume. [For 'Insiders'] we ended up getting ten photo doubles for it and then we just pulled every costume he had been in over all the years he has been with us, and I think we made three new ones. It was impossible to make twenty costumes because his are so elaborate!

"It's a wonderful series and we hope that it lives a long life in movies. It's so much fun to work on." Å

Stunts

Dan Shea

Dan Shea's history as *Stargate SG-1* stunt co-ordinator and sometime-recurring character Lieutenant Siler goes right back to the show's first year on air. As a result, for Shea the series' finale year was distinctly bittersweet. As usual his department pulled off some amazingly thrilling stunts – but every day at work following the announcement that year ten would be *Stargate SG-1's* last was tinged with sadness.

"It's a nasty feeling," says Shea candidly. "It was a two-pronged thing. First and foremost just your family – how are you going to eat? And then the second thing would be sadness for the series going."

Despite the worry that accompanied the end of the season, Shea reports that season ten allowed the stunts crew to create some of the most spectacular moments they had ever orchestrated.

"In that last season we actually did a lot of different stuff. We had a motorcycle chase [in 'Memento Mori'], which was pretty cool. We took over the whole of 91, which is a big production road in Vancouver, a whole highway. We had a special vehicle with camera mounts that could travel behind, in front of and beside the motorcycle at high speed, getting all these different cuts. We finished [with] this car roll called a nitrogen ram. The stunt guy has to lock up the brakes and turn the vehicle sideways and then he presses a button and a ram slams into the concrete and flips the car over. And he flipped over a bunch of times and landed in a ditch. In fact they tried the same gag on a big feature called *Rogue*, and they screwed up. They didn't get the car around, so it was a big huge gag that didn't work. But we made it work on our show!"

Shea's mention of the failure of a feature film in pulling off the same stunt is more than just professional pride. It serves to illustrate just how complicated such a sequence is; all the more so as the crew and director only have one chance to get it right.

"There's no second take and there's no rehearsing," Shea points out. "We were in a bit of a confined space in an isolated area out near the airport. It was a nice little intersection with nothing around, but it was a little bit tight, so it was really tough on the stunt driver. We put a bunch of sand on the ground because it was hot and the

Below: *Teal'c versus Mitchell in 'Talion', which featured some of the most spectacular stunts of the season.*

hot concrete would make it difficult for him to slide, and the car was so heavy and clunky. But he did a great job and it was perfect, he totally nailed it."

Other stunts did not go quite so smoothly. After ten years of shooting fights, falls and other fiascos, Shea was always on the lookout for ways to shoot stunts differently, and occasionally those efforts were not quite executed as expected.

Above: Browder gets a little help from Peter DeLuise during filming for 'Memento Mori'.

"In Peter DeLuise's episode, 'Memento Mori', we had these guys at the top of some crates and they had to do a high fall. So instead of just having the guy leave the shot [as usual] and not landing on shot, we had them leave the shot but we had a camera above. The stunt guy was about eight feet off the ground holding on, and just let himself go *boom!* onto the crates. Dust was flying up everywhere, and he actually hit the crates, which was a pretty cool shot. We've never actually done that, where we showed the landing. Then there was a similar gag in a show much later that Peter directed, ['Line in the Sand'], where this Ori soldier falls off a roof and he lands on a table. Ordinarily we have breakaway tables and legs and we score it. But instead of having it like WWE wrestling, where the guy hits the table and *boom!* it all explodes, we thought we wouldn't score it and we'd tilt the table slightly so when he hit it there would be some impact and then the table would fall over. But the guy hit it and the table didn't even go, so it was a nasty jolt to the stunt guy. But it was a really cool shot because our eyes, as viewers, are trained to see things break, but of course this didn't!" Å

Visual Effects

Michelle Comens

As a way to round out a decade of adventures, *Stargate SG-1*'s season ten had it all. And right from the get-go, as seen in 'Flesh and Blood', it was clear that the show's visual effects would outdo themselves for the finale season. Once again, the series' in-house department was expanded to allow for more sequences to be accomplished by the team supervised at Bridge Studios by Michelle Comens.

"It was a huge episode for us," Comens admits of the season opener, 'Flesh and Blood', "and luckily we had done a lot of the groundwork in 'Camelot'. We had the big mothership crashing into the Ori ship. That was our first huge ship blow-up that we'd really done here. It was on such a big scale and there was so much other work going on at the same time, so it was a big challenge, but we really pulled it off. It was all Robert Cooper's direction leading us on that. The good thing about doing a first episode like that is you have some more time to get going with it, because you're not in the middle of doing other episodes. So we started quite early, we did animatics and moving storyboards for the big set-up so we could start working on that even before the episode was shot. So while they were editing, we were starting to do all the modeling of the ships, the animation and texturing – getting all the simulations of how they're going to blow apart and that kind of thing."

Below: A Lucian Alliance vessel explodes against the shield of an Ori ship in 'Flesh and Blood'.

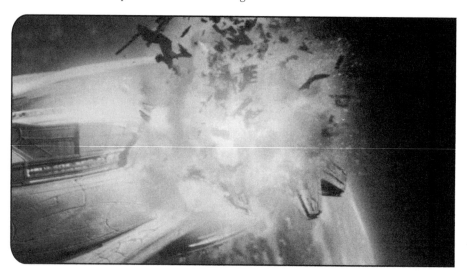

As in previous seasons, the department also utilized the talents of other visual effects vendors across Vancouver, specifically when it came to sequences involving the huge Ori fleet. However, as Comens explains, that sometimes presented its own challenges.

"We had two different companies work on them, so in 'Camelot' we had to really nail down [the look] because they're actually using different 3D [software] packages but the ships have to look exactly the same. It worked out though, I think."

One of the most intensive visual effects episodes of the season was the two hundredth episode. Coming in the middle of the season, the visual effects department had a huge task on their hands to accomplish everything the writers wanted to present in the celebratory episode. By this point in the show's year, the department is working on up to ten episodes at once, all in various stages of development from very early animatics and storyboards to those almost ready for final delivery to air.

"For us, one of the scariest things, which will sound kind of stupid," Comens laughs, "was all the puppet stuff. We shot all the plates, the background pieces with the actors, just for reference. Then we shot it without the actors, just with a background plate with nobody in it. Then we went down to LA and shot all the puppets on green screen with the same lenses, the same angles. They all had to fit perfectly and everything had to look as if they were actually in the set. So we were a bit worried about that."

Ironically, to make things a little easier for themselves, the crew decided to revert to a slightly lower-tech way of shooting this particular

Below: Team Stargate.

Visual Effects

Above: *Cheyenne*
Mountain explodes
in '200'.

sequence in the episode.

"We shot that on film," Comens explains. "Usually we shoot our entire show on HD cam, and that sequence we shot on film because it's a lot easier to key out a green screen on film. They wanted the look of the wires, [and] to keep something that small in the frame is really, really difficult. Luckily it was shot really well under controlled circumstances. It all went together perfectly so we were really, really happy with it. That was one big, scary headache for us," she laughs, "because if it didn't key well or something happened and we had to put back those wires all in 3D, it would have been a total nightmare."

"Cheyenne Mountain blowing up, that was the other huge thing," Comens continues. "[It] was just a little one-line thing in the script, but we had lots of discussion about how we were going to do it. We couldn't find a piece of stock footage that we could use, so we actually got a photographer down in that area to shoot us a new still of the mountain that we could actually blow up, and there were a whole bunch of different reference photos that we used. It was just as easy – nothing was moving and it was from a good wide distance so it doesn't really show up too much. We had quite a bit of delivery time on that episode, so it wasn't horrific, and once it all went together it was fine. It was a fun episode to work on, for sure. We had a good time."

Mid-season two-parter 'The Quest' afforded something completely new for the visual effects team to work on.

"The hardest thing for us in that episode is the huge CG creature we're working with – the dragon!" Comens laughs. "This one, luckily, we had a bit more time to work on. We did that in our in-house department here, and for a lot of people, getting a dragon is a big, fun thing to do! A lot of people do 3D character animation, and a creature like that is really fun. We had quite a bit of reference from the producers about what kind of dragon they wanted to see. There have been a lot of movies, so we could say, 'Oh, I like this dragon and I like this dragon...' We basically had it over here in 3D and everybody wanted to look at it and see what it was like. One aspect we had a lot of discussion about was actually the scale of it; how big it looks in certain scenes, and when you have someone else in the scenes. But to tell the truth it didn't go through tons and tons of evolution – we kind of nailed it and everyone was happy."

Incorporating such a large visual effects element into an episode such as this involves plenty of challenges on the set too.

"It was a hard episode to do," admits the visual effects supervisor. "Maybe not so hard to shoot, but hard to get all the pieces to go together afterwards! One of the difficult things for us is getting the actors to all have the same eyeline and all be looking the same way at the same big, imaginary creature. It's even hard for the editors, because you're tracking this big CG character – it's got to be outside, it's got to be in this big cave, it's got to breathe fire, it's got to be bursting out of a mountain. So it was

Above: The CG dragon in 'The Quest' was a huge test for visual effects.

Visual Effects

Above: *Mitchell looks on as Daniel assembles the super-weapon.*

challenging, but I think they did a really good job on it. We had two episodes to get it nailed down. Luckily, in 'The Quest, Part I' we only saw the dragon at the very end. The second one was the big one."

'The Quest' didn't only feature a big imaginary creature that had to be created from scratch. It also had several other visual effects elements that caused the team plenty of headaches, but that ultimately turned out well. One of these was Merlin's weapon. The weapon itself had actually already been visualized and built, but the script called for something akin to CGI retro-engineering for the sequence in which the device materializes and slots together piece by piece.

"Oh my god, that was actually a little bit of a nightmare!" Comens laughs. "It was pretty brutal! I actually stayed out of it a little bit – Krista McLean, who is our matte painter and playback supervisor, took that over. It's not playback but it has the same elements, in a way. They actually had a physical 3D piece that existed, but it was all the conceptual stuff of how the pieces float down and form that was always nebulous. People had different ideas of how it should look. Sometimes everybody gets on the same page, and then other times everyone has slightly different ideas, and then the more we go down different paths, the more different ideas get started and the more you have to write it in, so it can be difficult. It was one of the hardest things, and it sounds so silly. At the end of the concept planning it got really nailed down, but getting there was painful for

everybody involved, I think!"

Above: You don't
mess with Teal'c.

Another intensive episode was the season – and series – finale, 'Unending'. Set entirely in space, Comens reveals that her team relished the opportunity to use their talents in the most effective and yet subtle way possible.

"It was really fun to shoot. It was Robert Cooper directing and producing it [and] that actually makes it so much easier for us, just because you're not working with a director who has a different vision than the producer.

"When he's on the set, the whole time we're there he's telling us what he wants, and by the time we get into post, we've got everything really locked down in our heads – exactly what we're going to do. That episode was difficult, but it came together relatively easily. There were a few really challenging shots. Obviously the end sequence with the blowing up of the ship and Teal'c standing there, that was really difficult to put together. We're moving back on a dolly shot, moving in and out, and a lot of people think you just reverse it because we're basically pushing in on Teal'c and then we pull out. As we're pushing in, everything's blowing up and as we're pulling out we think everything's coming back together, but it's actually a continuous push-in. So it was really hard, and we had a dolly that wasn't really working properly that day," explains Comens, speaking of the camera rig used to film the shot, "so we had to do all this really intense 3D with this bouncy dolly that was really difficult to work with, so that was a challenge. It was pretty brutal." Å

Special Effects

Wray Douglas

Wray Douglas, *Stargate SG-1*'s special effects supervisor, can most often be found in his department's huge trailer, usually parked behind the effects stage of Bridge Studios. From here, Douglas and his team have, over the past decade, rustled up some of the biggest bouts of effects-driven destruction and carnage ever seen on the small screen. Exploding pyramids, firing staff weapons, gunfights, collapsing walls – you name it, if it involves fire, dust and debris, the special effects team are where it's at. For season ten, they created plenty of examples of all of the above – but most memorable, for Douglas at least, was the horde of marauding zombies that Mitchell battled in '200'.

"It was a lot of fun," he recalls. "We had hundreds and hundreds of bullet hits on all the zombies. It was a really dark hallway and it was very busy. There was a lot of blood and mayhem – it was good!"

Bullet hits constitute a very large part of what Douglas' team provides for *Stargate SG-1*, as every time someone fires a gun, a corresponding squib, or small explosion, must indicate where the bullet has hit. As one can imagine, it's a time-intensive job on a show where each script invariably involves the firing of a gun.

"For some of the zombies we had to make twenty or thirty hits per zombie, so there was a lot of work that went into it," Douglas agrees. "And you have to make it safe and make sure it won't hurt anybody by giving way in the face or hands or arms."

Each bullet hit is made on set in the effects trailer – clearly, a no-smoking area if ever there was one!

"There's a standard way for making bullet hits and blood hits for special effects. It's a small [cylinder] with TTN, which is an explosive powder, and you put a nichrome [conductive] wire to ignite it and set it off with an electrical charge," Douglas explains. "We have protective foam, and then an aluminum body-hit mortar which only projects a little explosion away from the stunt performer. [We add] a little tip and a holder of blood. It's taped onto the costume and set off electrically. Each one is made in the special effects trailer and then attached to the wardrobe. When there're numerous hits we have different systems for firing all

Below: When
zombies attack...

the bullet hits, whether they're firing themselves or remote controlled. It just depends on how many the director wants."

What's most impressive is the fact that each one of those squibs has to be set of individually – they can't be rigged to go off in a sequence so that Douglas' team can set an initial one off and let the others follow. Apart from anything else, that would cause safety issues, but it would also give the director less control over the set. Setting each bullet hit off separately means there's still a chance of calling cut mid-take, even if the camera is faced with a morass of flesh-eating dead guys.

"We have a special effects crew of up to sixteen people, and everybody works together in designing and building all the special effects," Douglas is keen to add. "We've been together for nine years, and we all work together very well as a team. There's no one person who designs and builds everything, we all do it together. Everybody has their own input. I think they're the best special effects team in Vancouver."

Though the conclusion of season ten meant the end of *Stargate SG-1*, Douglas's top-flight team survives. They are now working on sister show *Stargate: Atlantis*, which means the special effects trailer isn't going anywhere soon.

"When I finally got the word that *SG-1* was ending it was kind of sad, actually," Douglas admits. "It's been a really good show and a lot of these people have been on the show a really long time. You spend more time with these people than you do with your family." Λ

Above: *Cliff Simon demonstrates squibs in action.*

Production Design

James Robbins

J ames Robbins has been providing stunning conceptual artwork for the design department at *Stargate SG-1* since season six, lending his own distinct talent to the look and feel of the show. In year ten, Robbins extended his role to take on the task of designing the whole series, supervising the entire art department from initial artwork to the creation of the show's distinctive sets.

"The first ones we needed were for 'Flesh and Blood'," says Robbins of the standing sets he and his team created for the season. "We needed the interior of an Ori ship. In the previous season we ended up with Vala being abducted, and all of that was a virtual set. We had Claudia standing in a green set and everything you saw – the window and the edge of the ship and everything else – was all virtual. That set the standard for what the look was going to be, so I pretty much knew where I was going when we started. We went into Stage Three of our annex studio at Norco and built a run of corridors and rooms, one being the Oracle suite. The main thought behind it was big, dark and really had a sense of scale. We had a twenty feet by thirty feet room as the main room for the Oracle's suite, the corridors were about sixteen feet tall and the headers were nine feet tall. [They were] over-wide, as well, so you really got the sense that you were on a massive ship. They ended up scaling the Ori ships in VFX to roughly two kilometers long. Trying to emulate that on a sound stage that is ninety feet by a hundred feet is a bit of an issue," laughs the designer. "We didn't do any cheats with fake perspectives or anything, but we couldn't build a whole lot of corridors, so I tried to put little chicanes in so that every time you cut around a corridor you go somewhere else. I kept the hallways fairly spare so that it was a simple matter to change your access and it looks as if you are coming down a different part of the hallway. We built a couple of different pieces to put on the walls so we could change that out and, once again, you think you are in a different environment. It's actually the same thing I had to do in Stage Five of the SGC, because we're pretending it's twenty-eight storeys in there, and [we're] constantly shooting in the same corridors over and over again and changing out the pieces that are within it.

"But I think with some clever tricks with the camera and staging, 'Flesh and Blood' played out very well," continues the designer. "The thing was that we'd sort of gotten behind the eight ball a little bit and got in late with the design of the sets because there were some production issues at the beginning of the year. And we had seventeen days instead of the usual four to five weeks to pull that set together from the moment I put the drawings down and they were approved until we were shooting in it. So that's very much hats off to the construction and paint departments. They did a hell of a job!"

The Ori, as a relatively new design element, continued to evolve throughout the season, following the lead of what had already been established in season nine.

"They continue to grow," says Robbins, reflecting on the race's progress through the season, "because we are fleshing them out with every episode, we see different aspects. We developed the look of the Ori warriors and the Ori hierarchy with the Doci and the Priors when we first met them, and that set the feel for everything. I couldn't go in and do glass and stainless steel for these guys when they are walking around dressed in leathers and looking like a combination of a Roman and medieval look. I just follow a feel. When I'm drawing I know what the motif is in my head. I don't think anyone particularly says, 'We have to do this, we have to do that.'"

Another early season episode, 'Morpheus', provided plenty of exercise for the design team's ability to transform their already established sets into an unrecognizable setting. Rather than create a new set for the episode's

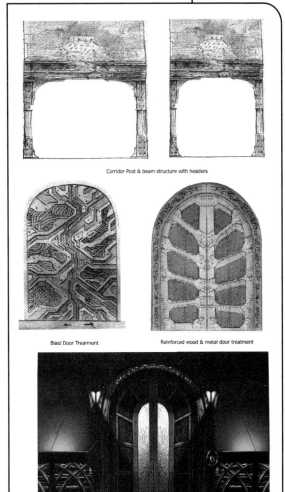

Corridor Post & beam structure with headers

Blast Door Treatment

Reinforced wood & metal door treatment

Standard door and wall treatment

Above: Plans for the elaborate Ori ship set.

environment, extensive redressing of the show's huge village set allowed the team to create an entirely new look inside the familiar space.

"'Morpheus' was quite an upgrade to the village that existed at the time," Robbins says. "I was in San Diego and was sitting having coffee one morning and drew the concept on a napkin. [I put] this aisle of trees down the center of what was to be this dead village, and they shot it all at night. They put up a big light at the end of the village to emulate the moonlight and did a nice wet-down and all these dead trees. The greens department just went wild. It was very successful, moody and eerie. That was quite a deal, but that was mostly for the greens department – they knocked themselves out for a week in there, turning that into the village of the dead."

One of the biggest challenges for Robbins in season ten was the huge task presented by the show's anniversary episode, '200'. The writers pulled out all the stops and put the characters in some particularly wacky places – and it was down to Robbins and his team to bring them to the screen.

"It was a lot of different builds just to take care of all the concepts that were put together," he recalls. "We had to emulate part of the *Daedalus* as part of the *Star Trek* engine room for Brad Wright's cameo in the Scotty-esque role! And the Furlings were in the show for just a moment, but that was a lot of design work from the visual effects of what their city looked like to what the interior of this lab that gets blown up looks like. The costumes themselves we actually produced ourselves in-house. Hats off to some of the brainiacs we have in our model shop, because they had the ears and eyes on servos and operated remote-control by a

Above: The mysteri-ous Furlings come to life.

little joystick. They were brilliant; they were really, really well done little critters. I did a couple of concepts and Rob Cooper said, 'Well, no, maybe they should look more like a koala bear or something,' and so that's

EPISODE
1002
MORPHEUS

VILLAGE
TREATMENT

ultimately where the look came from." Robbins chuckles at the memory. "Something as timid and cuddly as a koala bear and we ended up blowing them up!"

Fans also have Robbins to thank for some of the fantastic make-up designs apparent in the memorable 'zombies in Stargate Command' scenes.

"I created a couple of prosthetic looks for the zombie moment. The first one I did, Brad [Wright] reminded me that it's a show that actually goes out during the daytime," he laughs. "I had to pull back the concept from being quite so horrific. I went straight to *Night of the Living Dead*! So we prettied that up a little bit. It was quite funny."

When it came to filming the mid-season two-parter, 'The Quest', the team found themselves under the gun once more. The department had built a cave set several years before, but the sequence in which the team try to solve Merlin's riddles called for something far more elaborate – and for the action to intercut between the cave system and other settings entirely.

"The cave became such a huge presence. Before we could build anything for that episode we had to choreograph the movement through

Above: Robbins' design sketch for the "dead" village of Vagonbrei in 'Morpheus'.

Opposite top: An Ori warrior models the "Roman and medieval look".

Production Design

"Zoo"
♀ Zombie

1st pass - Too gorey

Above: *The first zombie sketches were rejected for being too gory.*

the existing corridors in the cave. [We looked at the] kind of change-outs we were going to have to do for them to find these plugs we'd put in so they could disappear. It was quite a deal choreographing that and making it work so you could get it all done in a shoot day. We walked it through and said, 'Okay, we're going to go from here to here.' They come up against a plaque that has an ancient riddle and then Daniel solves the riddle. What we do then is lock the camera off, everyone holds still, and we take the plug out and we continue on again and VFX do a little thing to assist in the disappearing. Recreating the environments that the cave warps to when Daniel starts playing with Merlin's device, we actually had to pull out the long central tunnel that was the interior of the cave. We removed it entirely and then put a winter set and a jungle or exterior wood set in there. The turnovers were done within days. There was very, very little time. The desert and winter was the same set with different color and we put some snow around. It was just about how clever you can be about making the right lighting choices and camera choices – and hopefully at the end of the day the audience isn't aware of it! When I finally saw the episodes, they were very successful considering they were such small sets."

Besides creating the look for the overall show, Robbins still found time to produce sketches for smaller details – for example, the design for the prosthetics worn by Michael Shanks in 'The Shroud'.

"I wanted to give him a slightly different version of the Priors' make-up," Robbins explains. "He wound up having a few more scarifications and swirls than most of them got. I think I did about three different versions of his make-up until we got what they were after. It was quite scary, actually," he laughs, "walking in to see Michael decked out like that. 'What happened to your eyes?' He was a trooper, he hung in there. Those kinds of things like the lenses are not comfortable to work in. If you're not used to wearing contacts at all it is quite a difficult thing.

"One of the bigger things that we had to take care of in that [episode] was Merlin's weapon itself, because it was assembled by visual effects, so that whole thing had to be made in stages. We started doing that in the previous episode and then he manages to finish assembling it in this episode, so they had to revisit the console that he was interfacing with in the cave and do another version of that with the ship."

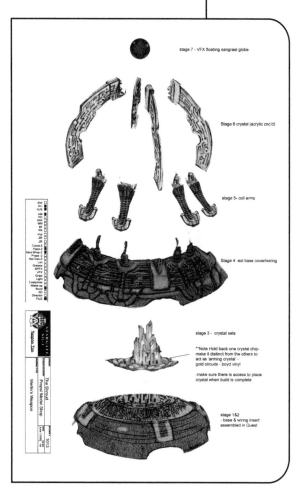

With the conclusion of the series as a regular concern, Robbins' work on the franchise continues as production designer for the feature-length *Stargate SG-1* productions and also for sister show *Stargate: Atlantis*. Regarding the end of the show, Robbins was perhaps somewhat more prepared than many of the other crew members, as he points out: "When I started season six on the show, season five was supposed to be the last year. So since I started, every year has been the last year! It was my first season as a designer for the show – the first whack at the bat, as it were. And I've been having a ball ever since!" Å

Above: *Merlin's weapon was so complex, it had to be created in different stages.*

Afterword

W hat to say? After ten years, you'd think something profound would come to mind, but truly… we've got nothing. You might expect that the conclusion of a series that we've spent the better part of our adult lives making would inspire us to write the mother of all afterwords, and that we would relish the opportunity to reflect on these ten seasons one last time. But the truth is, we're kind of reflected out. The two hundredth episode, *The Guinness Book of World Records* honoring us for becoming the longest running sci-fi show, and the eventual demise of *SG-1* as a series – surprisingly unexpected after so many years when it was actually planned for – all these events spurred us to reflect and wax poetic on the past.

Enough already. *Stargate* isn't over. We've completed two movies, and are planning two more. *Stargate: Atlantis* is still in production. There may even be a third series. If this were really the end of an era, we'd have packed up our offices by now. We're not done yet. We're still here. Time to stop eulogizing.

Stargate has always evolved. It evolved when we moved to the Sci Fi Channel, when Daniel ascended, and again when he came back. It evolved when O'Neill moved on, and Mitchell moved in. It will continue to evolve. There is only one thing that has never changed. Your support.

Without you, our constant viewers, our devoted fans, there would have been no ten years of *Stargate*. There would be no future for the franchise. So, for now, there is only one truly profound thing left to say about the past, the present, and the future.

Thank you.

Brad Wright and Robert C. Cooper
Vancouver, August 2007

ALSO AVAILABLE
FROM TITAN BOOKS

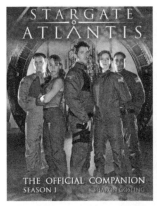

THE OFFICIAL COMPANION
SEASON 1 · SHARON GOSLING

THE OFFICIAL COMPANION
SEASON 2 · SHARON GOSLING

THE OFFICIAL COMPANION
SEASON 3 · SHARON GOSLING

COMING IN 2008!

THE OFFICIAL COMPANION
SEASON 4 · SHARON GOSLING

THE ILLUSTRATED COMPANION
SEASONS 1 AND 2 · Thomasina Gibson

THE ILLUSTRATED COMPANION
SEASONS 3 AND 4 · Thomasina Gibson

THE ILLUSTRATED COMPANION
SEASONS 5 AND 6 · Thomasina Gibson

THE ILLUSTRATED COMPANION
SEASONS 7 AND 8 · Thomasina Gibson

THE ILLUSTRATED COMPANION
SEASON 9 · Sharon Gosling

WWW.TITANBOOKS.COM